The Future of Profitability Models and Analysis for Law Firms

EDITED BY FRANCESCA RAMADAN

Commissioning editor
Alex Davies

Assistant commissioning editor
Francesca Ramadan

Published by
Globe Law and Business Ltd
3 Mylor Close
Horsell
Woking
Surrey GU21 4DD
United Kingdom
Tel: +44 20 3745 4770
www.globelawandbusiness.com

ISBN: 978-1-78358-372-0
A catalogue record for this book is available from the British Library

Contents

Executive summary

The convergence of changes in the legal landscape – wider economic pressures, the growing implementation of legal technologies, the disrupting influence of alternative service providers and their competitive pricing offerings – means that the corporatization of the law firm is well underway. The "business of law" is now more of a priority than ever before, with procurement and pricing professionals playing increasingly significant roles within firms, and a growing focus towards the measurement and analysis of profit, rather than simply its generation, becoming apparent. With this becoming common practice, it is now essential for those at the helm of their firm's profitability to take a deep dive into its real fundamentals. *The Future of Profitability Models and Analysis for Law Firms* is the latest publication to provide this kind of comprehensive exploration into the recent and revolutionary approaches firms are adopting in their pursuit of greater returns in this current period of renaissance for the law. Featuring contributions from field experts and thought leaders – including pricing directors, chief financial officers, and management consultants – *The Future of Profitability Models and Analysis for Law Firms* combines trendspotting, exploratory intelligence with case studies and real-world examples of best practice to act as a launchpad for application and instruction.

Law firms increasingly require attorneys to scope, plan, and budget matters on the front end, especially matters billed as an alternative fee arrangement. These plans and budgets are often used to set the price and project the profitability of matters, thereby controlling or mitigating the financial risk to the firm. Much attention is paid to getting the "right price" and packaging the value of the engagement so that the client recognizes the price as not only acceptable but completely justified. Getting the "right price" is hard, but executing the plan within the budget can be even harder. Monitoring performance to the budget on a regular basis for conformity and to reduce inefficiencies or working out of scope will, in turn, reduce write-downs and write-offs. This approach is an essential

– if often overlooked – step to executing within budget, particularly on fixed and capped fee matters. In chapter one, Dwight Floyd – chief pricing and value officer at Eversheds Sutherland – delves into this underappreciated but essential management tool, demonstrating how monitoring can promote awareness and communication at every stage of a matter.

The profession has come a long way since David Maister's 1984 article in *The American Lawyer*, where he set forth the logic for his net income per partner calculation. However, many law firms still utilize the classic metrics of personal productivity (fees collected off one's own work) and book of business (fees collected off one's own clients) to evaluate partner performance and billable hours for associates. It is important for firms to have a deeper understanding of what it costs to deliver its services and the profit contribution clients and practices make to the overall success of the firm. Chapter two, by James D Cotterman – principal at Altman Weil – provides an easily implemented framework to get started, which follows the cost-per-hour model that still dominates the profession. This chapter will also look into how profits are lost in the revenue cycle through pricing discounts, efficiency write-offs, and client valued write-downs.

The surprising truth about law firm profitability is that it is often not what you think. In chapter three, Eugenia Frenzel – director of pricing and practice management economics at Perkins Coie – discusses the need to shift focus from revenue to profitability in law firms of different sizes, and highlights emerging ways to accomplish that and go beyond. Even when profitability is fully embraced at a law firm, lawyers naturally and often purposefully gravitate toward lower net profit margins; at the same time, when it comes to the bottom line, law firms are notorious for keeping profitability as a back-office, behind-the-scenes metric. Moving profitability closer to center stage will reveal a paradigm shift and highlight the next challenge facing business operations in law firms.

In chapter four, Timothy Corcoran – former CEO turned management consultant – outlines the way in which law firms can leverage current market opportunities: understanding and embracing "traditional" profit measures, establishing the cost of an hour in an hourly billing world, and appreciating that profitability must include a far wider set of circumstances in a landscape where the continued prevalence of non-hourly fees and clients' relentless drive for efficiency means a profit model based on billing high rates and high hours is inherently limiting. Utilizing his expertise and insights from his practice, Timothy will delve into the disadvantages of idolizing one approach to profit and present a more multifaceted and comprehensive alternative.

Profitability reporting is essential for all law firms; however, it needs to move beyond a mandatory exercise to something that can proactively contribute to a firm's overall performance. In chapter five, Peter Lane Secor – chief pricing officer at Pepper Hamilton LLP – lays out his roadmap to effective profitability reporting, taking in its different aspects and incorporating them together into one cohesive strategy. Readers will learn new approaches to access and visibility, partner compensation statistics, and the importance of clear communication with key stakeholders.

Now that your firm has a matter and client profitability model, including revenue recognition and cost allocation methodologies, there is one more aspect to evaluate and address – partner compensation. Allocate too much as a matter cost and even minimal partner involvement can have a significant negative impact on performance; allocate too little and matters with the most partner involvement will see the highest margins. Partner involvement on its own should not be the driving factor for client or matter performance. Finding the right balance while being fair to partners and clients is a critical step to discerning accurate conclusions and incentivizing the right behaviors in your decision makers. What are other firms doing in this space? What are the strengths and blind-spots of the various approaches? These are questions that Ron Paquette – director of pricing at Akerman LLP – addresses in chapter six, providing vital guidance for those looking to learn from their competition in this space.

Companies consistently face challenges and opportunities to enhance their business models and provide value to their customers, workforce, and owners. Not surprisingly, law firms are no different. Chapter seven, by Thomas Van Der Moere – chief financial officer at Neal, Gerber & Eisenburg – focuses on a firm's opportunity to scrutinize existing and potential business using client and product profitability analysis, shifting the focus away from billable hours and time-measured revenue and providing insight that will allow a firm to direct its resources to areas where return can be maximized.

When the support of management has been achieved and a profit methodology established, what is to be done with the results? This is an issue delved into by Eddie Raychaudhuri – chief pricing and LPM officer – in chapter eight, as he utilizes his decade-long experience of launching and implementing law firm pricing initiatives to outline strategic approaches to improve firm financials. This will include setting goal metrics across differing practice groups, coaching partners on analyzing their books, and identifying which clients are tangibly beneficial for your firm's business.

Gathering data on a firm's profitability is a vital first step. The real value of this information, however, is when it contributes to an actionable strategy to improve revenue. In the final chapter, Madhav Srinivasan and Jim Foley – chief financial officer and pricing and legal project management director at Hunton Andrews Kurth LLP – delve into methods for leveraging profitability for action and results. This includes utilizing insights to realign timekeepers towards higher margin work, reorganizing staffing models that are linked to quality and financial results, and providing data and tools to partners to leverage in their practice.

About the authors

Tim Corcoran is a keynote speaker, consultant, author, and legal commentator. A former CEO with deep experience spanning three decades as a corporate executive, he guides law firm and law department leaders through the profitable disruption of outdated business models. As a change agent, Tim's focus is on helping law firms operationalize their strategy, with an emphasis on partner compensation, profitability, pricing, project management, and process improvement. Tim is a member of the Legal Marketing Association Hall of Fame and served as its 2014 President. He is a fellow and trustee of the College of Law Practice Management, and a sought-after speaker and writer on topics related to the changing business of law. Tim also authors the widely-read Corcoran's Business of Law blog.

James D Cotterman is a principal with Altman Weil, Inc. He advises law firms on compensation, capital structure, and other economic issues, governance, management, and law firm merger assessments. Before joining Altman Weil in 1988, Mr Cotterman was manager of acquisitions for a public company in the healthcare industry, where he developed, evaluated, negotiated and integrated merger opportunities. Mr Cotterman is the author of *Cotterman on Compensation*, a blog on lawyer compensation and law firm finance. He is the lead author of the ABA book *Compensation Plans for Law Firms*, and is a member of the Board of Editors of *Accounting and Financial Planning for Law Firms*. He has been the supervising author for Matthew Bender's loose-leaf text *How to Manage Your Law Office*. His writings have appeared in *The American Lawyer*, *The National Law Journal*, ABA's *Law Practice*, *International Law Firm Management* and many other publications. Mr Cotterman is a frequent speaker and lecturer, including presentations for annual and regional conferences of the American Bar Association and the Association of Legal Administrators, as well as numerous state and local Bar and ALA meetings. He is a fellow of the College of Law Practice Management.

Dwight Floyd is the chief pricing and value officer at Eversheds Sutherland (US) LLP. Dwight and his team work with Eversheds Sutherland attorneys and clients to provide superior value by developing and implementing creative pricing and service delivery strategies. Dwight is a former litigation partner and a biologist who brings a different approach to common challenges in the legal market. As in our natural ecosystem, he recognizes that everything in the legal ecosystem is connected to everything else. His challenge is discovering and revealing to attorneys and clients how those connections can benefit and sustain everyone involved while still conserving resources. Dwight is rated AV by Martindale-Hubbell and is an Accredited Legal Pricing Professional (ALPP) by the True Value Partnering Institute. He received his JD from the University of Virginia School of Law, his MS from Colorado State University, and his BS from Clemson University.

Jim Foley is the pricing and legal project management director at Hunton Andrews Kurth LLP, where he oversees the pricing, legal project management, matter analytics, business intake and conflicts areas. He has extensive experience in alternative fee arrangements (AFAs), legal project management (LPM), matter budgeting, law firm financial management, and financial analysis. Jim was formerly the mayor of Ashland, Virginia.

Eugenia Frenzel is the director of pricing and practice management economics at Perkins Coie LLP, focusing on forging and strengthening lasting client relationships through tailored pricing, effective matter management, and synergistic collaboration. She strives to deliver innovative business solutions to internal and external clients. With over 15 years of legal operations expertise at three AmLaw 50 firms, Eugenia is passionate about ensuring organizational strategic agility in today's fast paced and often volatile environment. Eugenia is an accredited legal pricing professional, a regular speaker at industry conferences, and a volunteer with ILTA. She is a licensed attorney and received her JD from Quinnipiac University School of Law; Eugenia received both her MS in Organizational Leadership and BS in Business from Mercy College.

Peter Lane Secor is the chief pricing officer at Pepper Hamilton LLP. Peter concentrates on legal project management with a focus on improving efficiencies through shared management responsibilities, strengthening communication, and making value transparent. His expertise includes client/matter profit analysis and providing partners with performance evaluations from a financial perspective.

Ron Paquette is the director of pricing at Akerman LLP, an Amlaw 100 firm with over 700 lawyers and professionals across 24 offices in the US. He has over 13 years of legal finance and client/matter profitability experience with prior roles as both a vendor/consultant and in-house at two other large law firms. His four years with Redwood Analytics were primarily spent focused on new analytic methodologies for the industry, exposing him to a wide array of approaches to client/matter profitability and their underlying strengths and weaknesses. He took this experience in-house, where he has implemented or improved profitability models in each firm. In his current role, Ron is rolling out profitability with the Akerman partnership while also implementing the required processes and disciplines for a robust and proactive pricing organization.

Eddie Raychaudhuri has over a decade of experience launching and implementing pricing and LPM initiatives at law firms, which incorporates process improvement, practice innovation, alternative staffing, client fee negotiations, establishing profit methodologies, and developing fee arrangements and monitoring fee deals. Eddie has a proven track record of working with practice groups to optimize practice platforms, business performance, client relationships, and operations to achieve increased profitability and reduce institutional risks while maximizing client value. Eddie earned his JD/MBA from Case Western Reserve University School of Law and American University's Kogod School of Business.

Madhav Srinivasan is the chief financial officer at Hunton Andrews Kurth LLP, leading the global finance and pricing competencies. Madhav is an ALM Intelligence Fellow and also an adjunct faculty at Columbia Law School in New York and University of Texas at Austin School of Law. He is a published author and frequent speaker at major conferences.

Thomas Van Der Moere is the chief financial officer at Neal, Gerber & Eisenberg LLP, a Chicago-based law firm with over 140 lawyers, where he oversees the financial operations of the firm including the areas of accounting, treasury management, planning/analytics/business intelligence, practice economics and strategic pricing, financial systems, and new business acceptance and risk management. Tom has expertise in professional service firm administrative and financial management, performance and compensation analysis, financial and operational analysis and modeling, strategic planning, process development and re-engineering, firm/project profitability and risk management, and business intelligence. He also has significant financial experience with public and private companies in professional services, energy, and manufacturing industries. Tom has an MBA from the University of Chicago Booth School of Business and an MS in Accounting and Business Management from the University of Tulsa.

Chapter 1:
Write-downs, discounts, and that pesky red queen – finding profit by budgeting and monitoring matters

By Dwight Floyd, chief pricing and value officer, Eversheds Sutherland (US) LLP

The (improbable) proposition

What if I said you could save five to ten percent of your revenue next year and add it directly to your bottom line with minimal effort? That you could increase your profits by ten to 20 percent? What if I told you this was possible simply by paying attention to what you are doing? Would you do it? Does your firm culture allow it? Does it promote it?

The (persistent) problem

The notice comes to the pricing director through the workflow at 8:10am:

> PARTNER WRITE-DOWN REQUEST EXCEEDS AUTHORITY. ADDITIONAL APPROVALS REQUIRED. WRITE-DOWN AMOUNT REQUESTED: $254,489.

At 8:12am the pricing director's phone rings. It is the managing partner:

"What in the world is going on?!? A quarter of a million dollar write-down?!? How did this happen? What are our options? And how can we keep this from happening again?"

The pricing director calls the rainmaker partner supervising the matter and hears a familiar story:

"The matter was referred to us by a lawyer at another firm who had quoted them a price but was conflicted out. We thought the price was a little low, but the client thought it was right and wanted it as a fixed fee. Remember now, this is a client we have really wanted to get work from and we have a chance for a lot of work in the future, so we bumped the price up a tiny bit and agreed to fix the fee. Don't you remember? We worked through all this and the budget last year."

"Oh," says the pricing director, "*that* matter. I remember all those risks and assumptions you pointed out. There were some other parties you thought would join and the judge was squirrely. We were going to scope around the biggest issues and make some clear assumptions in the document. I never heard anything more after we worked up a draft. It never went through the approval process. Is *that* the matter?"

"Yeah – that one. We didn't want to spook the client, so we gave them the basic scope and said we'd do the fixed fee, but, in the meantime, we'd bill it hourly up to the fee. Of course now we're over the cap. That's what we need to write down."

The pricing director bites his tongue about the fixed fee worked like a cap and the entire AFA offering without proper approvals:

"Why did it go over the cap?"

"Well," the partner's voice trails off. "You see we had an associate or two doing some research and they went down some rabbit holes they didn't need to, so that was part of it; and then we had a bunch of time that couldn't be billed because somebody – you know who I'm talking about – didn't enter his time for more than a month and the billing system will reject all of it! That's about $50K, the rest of it is because the whole case changed. Those other parties we talked about – they all joined and they asserted new claims and we had to put in new defenses, and the judge made us do some things we didn't expect. Naturally we had to do all these things for the benefit of the client. We *had* to!"

"Did you discuss the scope change with the client? Or how it would affect the price?"

"No – but they knew what was going on, and we didn't want to alarm them or make them think we didn't know what was coming. Plus we budgeted for just such a circumstance. We built in a little cushion."

"But…?"

"But… we exceeded the cushion by $254,489."

"When did you realize this?"

"Oh, we knew pretty quickly. I knew it right away when I was looking at that last pre-bill."

This all sounds like a pricing director's (and managing partner's) nightmare. A quarter of a million dollar write-down is real money in anyone's book, but we do not have nearly enough information to judge how bad this situation is. If, for example, the negotiated cap was $5m and it was billed at standard rates up to the cap, the write-down would amount to a five percent discount off standard. It is not ideal, but most firms would not lose much sleep over a five percent discount.

However, if the cap was at $1m, the $250K write-down amounts to a 20 percent discount – enough to give anyone pause. Because every dollar of discount comes straight from the bottom line, a 20 percent discount could come close to giving away all your profit or, at least, severely reducing the margin.[1] Because this partner did not follow best practices, we do not know exactly how the matter was set up, which hours have been billed at standard, and which hours are being written down. Some of these hours may be more expensive than others.

The problem, however, is not the numbers themselves; it is the fact that no one seems to know precisely what is going on. That lack of knowledge and the missteps it causes are inevitably accounted for in the write-down.

Why should I care?

Much has been written recently about the decreasing realization of the modern American law firm, including Thomson Reuters' 2018 Dynamic Law Firms Study[2] and Roy Strom's article in *The American Lawyer*, "How the Am Law 100 Left $4.4B on the Table in 2018".[3] The common refrain is that while firms have made some headway in increasing standard rates,[4] clients have continued to push for greater and greater discounts. Firms that barely considered discounting in the past suddenly find themselves forced to make at least some discounted offerings as table stakes in elaborate RFPs for panel participation. As a result, firms expend considerable resources to forecast and model the effects of these set discounts on their revenue and profits.

Tempting as it is to cite the Red Queen Hypothesis of evolutionary biology and/or the general nature of zero-sum games in economic and ecological theory, and to rail against the wastefulness of investing in an unnecessary arms race, instead let us simply assume, for the sake of this argument, that annual rate increases roughly offset the annual decreases in realization. This may not be precisely, mathematically, true. In fact, at any point in time, it is likely to lean (sometimes heavily) in favor of client or law firm. The point is to recognize that there are two strong antagonistic pressures – one for decreases and one for increases – acting within this system. Said another way, let us assume that firms' rates are increasing more to roughly match the increased discounting pressure from clients and vice versa to create a rough sort of equilibrium.

If this premise is true, it would be incorrect to assume that the entire loss in realization is "left on the table," because we are measuring against the wrong theoretical maximum. That maximum, the result of the (near) zero-sum game, includes some measure of inflation to account for the inflated discounting pressure. It is the rare firm that expects or measures itself strictly against 100 percent realization. (In fact, if it achieved 100 percent, it almost certainly has rates that are too low because it is never getting any pushback. No client is ever refusing to pay.) The real standard for attainable realization, then, is indeterminate but somewhere south of 100 percent.

That is not to say that the negotiated discount portion of lower realization should be ignored. On the contrary, it tends to command almost all of our attention because the clients present it to us directly and it takes so much energy to maintain some semblance of equilibrium. It is the front line of pricing, and it is one of the main reasons pricing professionals exist – to help maintain competitive rates in the face of ever-increasing client headwinds for lower rates and discounts. We are, to paraphrase the Red Queen, running as fast as we possibly can just to stand still.

Meanwhile, there is another distinct subset of decreased realization that is often ignored and where the Red Queen does not rule. It represents an additional discount over which the client has little, if any, control or knowledge. It is the revenue leakage *we allow* – the additional discount that *we give* – and of which the client is often not aware for, among other things, working out of scope, working inefficiently, working inappropriate timekeepers, practicing poor timekeeping hygiene, and failing to work to budget. It is the writing down of billable time because it "cannot be billed". This subset of realization is the true "money left on the table," or, more accurately, it is money that should never have been on the table. It is a measure of the law firm's mistakes, missteps, and miscalculations.

Whether or not discounting and standard rate setting is a zero-sum game, if we price that first part of the realization equation – the negotiated discount – correctly (i.e., profitably and efficiently within the market),[5] then *that* becomes the baseline against which to measure matters. Every dollar we prevent from leaking from that price – every dollar that is retained – contributes to maintaining the predicted profitability for that matter. Every dollar leaked or written down reduces the profit by the same dollar because the costs of production are fixed.[6]

Brief (scoffing) interlude

This stuff is obvious. Of course we should not be wasteful, but this is peanuts compared to the discounting pressure, right? Why are we even discussing this? How much is really at stake? How much can be gained here? Where is that 20 percent increase in profits you promised?!

Why should I care? (continued)

For all the data circulated about overall realization and its trends, there is relatively little describing this subset of the profitability waterfall. Bill Josten, strategic content manager for the Thomson Reuters Legal Executive Institute, relying on the 2018 Dynamic Law Firms Study and Peer Monitor data, estimates that firms leak from 7.0-8.4 percent in value from worked value to billed value. Colin Jasper and Stuart Dodds of Positive Pricing have seen a similar, if slightly broader, range of five to ten percent. An unscientific survey of pricing professionals at leading law firms supports the same general range. Regardless of a firm's revenue level, retaining five to ten percent and adding it to the firm's bottom line and to each partner's is a significant number. Assuming a 30 percent operating margin, adding five to ten percent of revenue straight to the bottom line would increase the operating margin by 11-21 percent.

Plus, if the average negotiated discount from standard is in virtually the same seven to nine percent range, should we not be devoting as much attention to correcting it, especially when it is entirely within our control and when there is no client pushback? Will our results not be better as a matter of course?

Turning back to our original "nightmare" write-down scenario, if the matter was budgeted and billed as a cap of $1m and that budget, after fully allocating costs and expenses, was expected to yield a margin of $300k (30 percent), then writing down the $250k would be painful, but, at least, some profit would remain. Overall, the effective rate on the matter would likely drop, depending on the distribution of work. If the overage happened to be more expensive and at a slimmer margin, say 12 percent because more expensive timekeepers worked it, then the overall margin would drop even more.

Solution – a little bit can go a long way (just do *something*)

The lost revenue in these write-downs is, essentially, a representation of waste in the firm's work process. Following the principles of lean manufacturing, these write-downs fall into at least three of the seven types of waste:

- Over production – producing more than is needed before it is needed;
- Over processing – doing more work than is necessary; and
- Defects – lost work or rework.

For the process oriented among us, this type of waste may scream for some sort of project management or formalized legal project management. That would almost certainly help. However, for firm cultures where those approaches are not yet embedded, the barriers to entry for many attorneys are (or are perceived to be) high. A cynical attorney might even suggest that the cost to implement and maintain such a formal program, combined with the administrative costs of the attorneys will approach the five to ten percent range, thus nullifying its effect.

The benefits of LPM are extolled in depth by leaders in this field (see further reading below), and it is beyond the scope of this chapter to quantify its demonstrated benefits.

Undoubtedly, though, even without a full-fledged program, *some modicum of matter management will necessarily produce real results.* Without arguing the return on investment of formal LPM programs, it should be incontrovertible that even a little measurement and management is better than none. Call it basic matter management, LPM-lite, or just old-fashioned lawyering, if an attorney has scoped, planned, and budgeted a matter and, at any given time, knows who is doing what and how it relates to the overall budget, that attorney will almost certainly reduce write-downs. That is no great revelation.

For example, if an associate has spent 15 hours on something that should have taken ten, the partner can discuss the issue and determine whether the associate should stop. Yes, there may still be five hours written down, but that is better than 15, 20, or 50 wasted hours. Plus, with a quick conversation, the partner has set the tone for the entire matter and future matters. The associate knows that everyone is being held to the budget and is more likely to discuss it earlier, thereby creating a positive feedback loop.

This feedback loop and control mechanism can be set up in a variety of ways and at a number of places in the matter lifecycle:

- Establish processes and controls for matters (especially riskier matters) to be (1) reviewed and approved by stakeholders; (2) tagged appropriately in the system; and (3) monitored throughout their lifecycles;

- Work with the client and internal team to fully scope the matter;
- Plan the matter, including the identification of risks and assigning resources;
- Build a budget that reflects the plan (it need not be perfect); and
- Execute the plan to budget by frequent monitoring.

This last step is, arguably, the most important and often the most overlooked. It does not have to be elaborate or perfect. It can be as simple as running a report, an early pre-bill, from your time and billing system every week or two rather than once a month. If you have good data analysts or reporting gurus in your accounting department, they may run an automated report or even set up alerts for certain events. (This is all doable whether or not you are using phase and task codes.) There are also software packages that can compare performance to budget and display it in real-time or near real-time to working attorneys, supervising attorneys, or even the client. Doing something – anything – at any one of these steps is better than doing none.

Ultimately, though, more people, more processes, or more technology will not solve this challenge. It is a cultural shift where this level of waste and the concomitant lost earnings is tolerated or where every owner of the business pays attention to those losses and does what can be done to reduce or eliminate them. To that end, firm-level KPIs that focus on "write-downs" or "additional discounts" or "profitability" in addition to the more traditional focus on "billings," "collections," and "utilization" will emphasize to partners the importance of these efforts and that those ideals are now a part of the culture of the firm. You can even build KPIs around time to post and time to bill to promote good timekeeping hygiene – a bore, to be sure, but a bore that ties directly to write-downs and lost revenue.

At the risk of oversimplifying the issues, the best solution to decrease write-downs and recapture this leaking revenue is to do *something*. Do not wait for the perfect opportunity. Do not wait until the right people or the right technologies are in place. Do not stop improving improving, and do not let perfection be the enemy of the good. Do something today. Simply *talking* about it will move the needle. Doing any one or more of the things described here can yield results in as little as a few months.

Do it. It may be the easiest way to escape the Red Queen.

Further reading

Susan Raridon Lambreth and David A. Rueff Jr., *The Power of Legal Project Management: A Practical Handbook* (2014), American Bar Association.
Stuart J. T. Dodds, *Smarter Pricing, Smarter Profit* (2014), American Bar Association.
Jim Hassett, Mike Egnatchik et al., *The Legal Project Management Quick Reference Guide: Tools and templates to increase efficiency* (4th ed. 2016), LegalBizDev.

References

1. Assuming a 30 percent operating margin after allocating all fixed costs (i.e. before equity distribution).
2. http://images.ask.legalsolutions.thomsonreuters.com/Web/TRlegalUS/%7Ba5663eb9-7ba1-43c3-a742-b0a869709dae%7D_S072157.pdf
3. www.law.com/americanlawyer/2019/04/23/clients-are-demanding-discounts-and-leaving-law-firms-at-a-loss/
4. For purposes of this chapter, "standard rates" are the rack rates charged for an hour of time with no discounting or other arrangement. The generic term "rates" includes but is not limited to a charge rate per hour. It also includes "effective rates" as a result of AFAs of any size or shape and/or the result of any discounting. It is, simply, the measure of revenue for each unit of production cost expended.
5. This is more fully discussed elsewhere in this book.
6. This assumes some firmwide utilization optimum and that those lost hours would be put into production elsewhere. It recognizes that each hour (and dollar) lost in one matter represents lost opportunity cost from another.

Chapter 2:
Calculating profitability

By James D Cotterman, principal, Altman Weil

Law firms are investing in more sophisticated measures to understand where and how they make money. The profession has come a long way from David Maister's 1984 article in *The American Lawyer* where he defined profitability as follows:

NIPP = (1 + L) x (BR) x (U) x (R) x (M)

NIPP = Net Income Per Partner

L = Leverage

BR = Billing Rate

U = Utilization (client billable hours recorded)

R = Realization (fees collected divided by the "standard value" of time recorded)

M = Margin (net income divided by fees collected)

For decades after Maister's defining piece, law firms continued to focus on fees collected for the two most touted performance metrics – personal productivity (fees collected off one's own work) and book of business (fees collected off one's own clients). Billable hours usually came into the mix around the middle for partners, but key for associates, on the scale of compensation factors.

The simplicity of this assessment worked well for several reasons. Law firms were generally rooted in a shared philosophy and had similar practices/clients. For these firms the economics and operating style of one practice versus another (within each firm) were not significantly different enough to warrant closer examination. The collegial nature of law firm partnerships also made this methodology popular. Scrutiny of each practice and client can be a divisive issue. In addition, law firm partners generally are not well schooled in finance and accounting, so delving into cost allocations is outside their comfort zone. Finally, for many years the financial systems used by law firms were not robust and sophisticated enough to undertake a more in-depth analysis.

Much changes with the passage of time. Law firms mature. Individual practices travel different paths resulting over time in quite different economics. Law firms grow, adding new partners, practices, and clients. Each addition changes the firm, and how well these additions fit together present new strategic, cultural, and financial considerations. Today the profession has sophisticated financial tools and expert financial staff to develop and analyze metrics. Moreover, the post-recession legal market has brought increased competition among lawyers/firms and clients who are more aggressive in seeking discounts and/or alternate pricing methods.

Getting started – developing assumptions

A deeper understanding of profitability will have an impact on firm operations. It will affect hiring and retention of personnel and the selection and retention of clients. It will affect promotion and compensation decisions. It will affect engagement pricing. It will affect the delivery of legal services with the underlying premise of efficiency likely becoming as important a consideration as quality and speed of service.

If you are just getting started in profitability analysis, I recommend that you begin with the simplest tools. It is better to have something that aids decision-making than to struggle with too much theory and attempts at elegant precision. The first tool to develop is a means to match expenses to revenue – answering the basic question of what does it cost to generate the fee? Add refinement and complexity to the analysis with experience. The following simple approach uses overall firm overhead with no sub-allocations of expenses. Some assumptions are used that will aid the reader in applying this method in their own firm. The assumptions are:

- A single office law firm partnership with a collection of practices that are reasonably similar in their economic models;
- Partners and associates use/share resources (offices, secretaries, technology and the like) without any significant distinction from group to group. This means that office sizes are very similar,

secretarial sharing is similar across groups, and all timekeepers use a similar technology package;

- Paralegal use/sharing of resources is about one-half that of lawyers. Thus, count each lawyer as one fee-earner and each paralegal as one-half a fee-earner. This is the convention commonly found in most economic surveys of the profession;
- Expenses include the net effect of cost advances and recoveries on behalf of clients; and
- Compensation is deducted from total expenses to determine firm overhead. Define compensation as salary, bonus, benefits, and associated payroll taxes.

Accordingly, we can take the total expenses of the law firm and subtract the compensation costs of the employed timekeepers (generally the associates and paralegals). The remaining expenses represent the overhead of the firm. Divide this remainder by the total full-time-equivalent (FTE) fee-earners to determine the overhead per fee-earner.

Factoring compensation expenses

Next, we deal with compensation expenses. There are three assumptions for this exercise:

- We are looking for hourly cost rates for each group of individuals – equity partners, non-equity partners, associates and paralegals – so average compensation for each group is used;
- Compensation for development of hourly cost rates generally includes only salary, benefits, and the associated payroll taxes. Including bonuses (with their associated benefit and payroll tax costs) is an option depending on your firm's particular philosophy on bonuses. A bonus paid only when an individual's performance exceeds expected levels is properly excluded. If your firm pays a bonus for performance at or below expectations (profit sharing – not the 401(k) type, or simply a deferred salary or holdback) then at least that aspect of the bonus is rightly included in this analysis. Keep it simple and go with all or no bonuses – remember we are aiming for simplicity. History provides actual data. Current year analysis will require using the assumptions and estimates from the firm's budget; and

- A partner's compensation consists of a fair exchange for his/her labor (the portion we need) and the profits earned on the work done by others (the portion to exclude). There may also be a return on capital component depending on whether the firm pays interest on partner capital or not. Again, for simplification, we will use the partners' draw (cash plus benefits paid separately by the firm) as a proxy for the fair exchange portion we are interested in for our purposes. The likely result is excluding 25-40 percent of a partner's compensation from this analysis. Other proxies that could be substituted include extending the lock-step associate pay scale into the partner ranks or using an outside reference point such as a senior in-house lawyer.

Developing cost rates

We now have the total average cost of each group to include:

- Allocated overhead;
- Base pay;
- Planned bonuses; and
- Benefits and taxes.

Divide the total average cost by the expected billable hours to obtain an hourly cost rate. Divide that rate by the expected realization factor for the group to obtain a required internal hourly rate. This is the lowest breakeven rate after considering revenue leakage (discussed later). Divide by an expected profit margin to obtain a target billing rate. A sample calculation is shown in Figure 1.

The sample calculation tells the user that for the firm to cover its costs it must net $163 per hour on an average associate. To account for revenue leaks (discussed later) it must set the average associate rate no lower than $199 per hour. Finally, if the firm wants to earn a profit on the associate it must set an even higher rate. With the average associate yielding a 22 percent profit margin, that rate is $255 per hour.

The underlying data for the above sample calculations are averages from publicly available surveys. To prove the analysis, we compared the calculated target billing rates to the survey data for standard billing rates. They matched within rounding conventions.

	Total	Equity	Non-equity	Associates	Paralegals
Firm-wide					
Total expenses	$36,801,000				
Less lawyer compensation	$15,249,000				
Less paralegal compensation	$1,752,000				
Firm overhead	$19,800,000				
Total FTE timekeepers		50.00	25.00	45.00	24.00
Total FTE fee-earners	132.00	50.00	25.00	45.00	12.00
Overhead per fee earner	$150,000				
Per individual group					
Allocated overhead		$150,000	$150,000	$150,000	$75,000
Salary/Draw		$500,000	$250,000	$115,000	$60,000
Planned performance bonus		$0	$25,000	$6,000	$0
Benefits and taxes		$0	$49,500	$14,500	$9,500
Total cost before any additional bonuses		$650,000	$474,500	$285,500	$144,500
Expected billable hours		1,700	1,550	1,750	1,450
Cost rate		$382	$306	$163	$100
Expected realization		88%	86%	82%	80%
Required Internal hourly rate		$434	$356	$199	$125
Expected profit margin		10%	15%	22%	34%
Expected profit		$72,200	$83,700	$80,500	$74,400
Target billing rate		$485	$420	$255	$190

Figure 1

Refining the simple analysis

This approach can be refined in a number of ways while preserving much of its simplicity. The first is to weight the allocation of general overhead differently. Some firms may decide that partners absorb a greater proportion of the overhead than associates do. For example, a firm may assign an equity partner a fee-earner equivalency of say 1.50, non-equity partners 1.25, senior associates 1.0, junior associates 0.75 and paralegals remaining 0.50. The variations on this theme are vast. What is important is a sense that the allocation reasonably reflects reality and is revisited periodically to recheck the assumptions.

The next refinement is to sub-divide the very broad groupings of equity and non-equity partners, associates and paralegals by practice area. General overhead would remain the same. However, compensation levels and billable hour expectations would likely vary, affecting the resulting hourly rates.

Another refinement could be to divide the associates by class year or class groupings (first and second years, third and fourth years and so on). Each of these refinements yields more tailored information. Finally, it is possible to create an internal rate calculation for each timekeeper. In such cases, the compensation and billable hour expectations are unique to a single person, while the allocated overhead is the common number shared by all.

Many firms will choose to combine their approaches. At the partner level, where compensation differences are often quite significant, setting individual cost rates makes a great deal of sense. Concurrently the firm may obtain reasonably useful data using class year or some lesser distinction at the associate level.

Some firms will take the rapidly evolving role of secretaries out of general overhead and apportion them more directly based on what that firm is doing in this area. Such special allocations will reflect the vastly different use of legal secretaries by timekeeper age cohort and practice specialty.

Multi-office firms will probably want to allocate office-specific costs directly. In those instances, it is necessary to divide the main office into its operations unit and its administrative services unit. Administrative services are those activities (human resources, finance, technology and the like) that serve the entire firm along with their associated housing costs. These costs are allocated across all timekeepers firm-wide.

It may be appropriate to briefly state that it is possible to devise a cost accounting system so detailed as to take any activity and assign it to multiple cost centers – each of the aforementioned sub-groups. The account numbering schematic for such a system would be quite complex, as would the coding and verification tasks. We will forgo the obvious political challenges involved in selling such a complex system. Therefore, while precision is a possibility, it is largely not a practical approach.

Allocating costs to revenue

Once the cost rates are settled, one can move on to allocating costs. This requires applying the appropriate cost rates to each timekeeper and allowing the financial software to flow costs throughout the system (timekeeper, class, timekeeper status, task, matter, matter type, client, client industry, practice area, department, and office). The cost rates will follow the recorded hours based on the coding profiles established when a matter is opened and when time is recorded.

If your timekeepers are disciplined time recorders, it is possible to learn much about how legal services are delivered – from leverage employed to costs incurred to timing of tasks to variability of results. This information (accurate hourly histories and reasoned cost data) can help you to price non-hourly projects.

In some firms, the timekeepers do not record time well or perhaps not at all. In these instances, it may be necessary to allocate costs to an assigned practice area, office, or billing lawyer, depending on how your firm is organized. Thus, cost rates on an hourly basis are not used. The ability to look at client and matter profitability is lost, but overall portfolios, practice areas, and office data may still be relevant.

Profitability can then be determined by comparing the fee receipts to the costs assigned under each tracking category – timekeeper, class, matter, client, practice area and the like. I have avoided getting into accounting technicalities, but here it is important to discuss cash and accrual basis accounting. Law firms primarily operate as cash businesses. Revenues are reported as cash is collected and expenses are recognized as cash is disbursed.[1]

Remember that the cost rates developed earlier are based on expected billable time recorded. Thus, the best match of expenses to revenues is to let the cost rates flow from recorded billable hours (Figure 2).

So, we now have a simple model that aids us in understanding the basic relationships of costs to fees collected. However, this very simple approach to examining profitability does not isolate important factors that affect how well your firm is operating. The next refinement to take on is a closer examination of the variables associated with fees collected.

	Total	Equity	Non-equity	Associates	Paralegals
Fee collections	$125,033	$21,453	$36,006	$52,326	$15,249
Allocated Expenses					
Cost rate	$201	$382	$306	$163	$100
Hours	500	50	100	250	100
Allocated cost of services rendered	$100,482	$19,118	$30,613	$40,786	$9,966
Profit before carrying costs	$24,551	$2,335	$5,393	$11,540	$5,283
Margin before carrying costs	19.6%	10.9%	15.0%	22.1%	34.6%

Figure 2

Warehousing labor

Before moving on, I want to touch on another profitability issue affecting revenue – overcapacity or warehoused labor. The profession used to expect a certain productivity level across its timekeepers – e.g., for equity partners 1,650 billable hours, for non-equity partners 1,750 billable hours, and for associates 1,850 billable hours. Unfortunately, the profession has not held to that standard for many years, resulting in increasing levels of overcapacity.

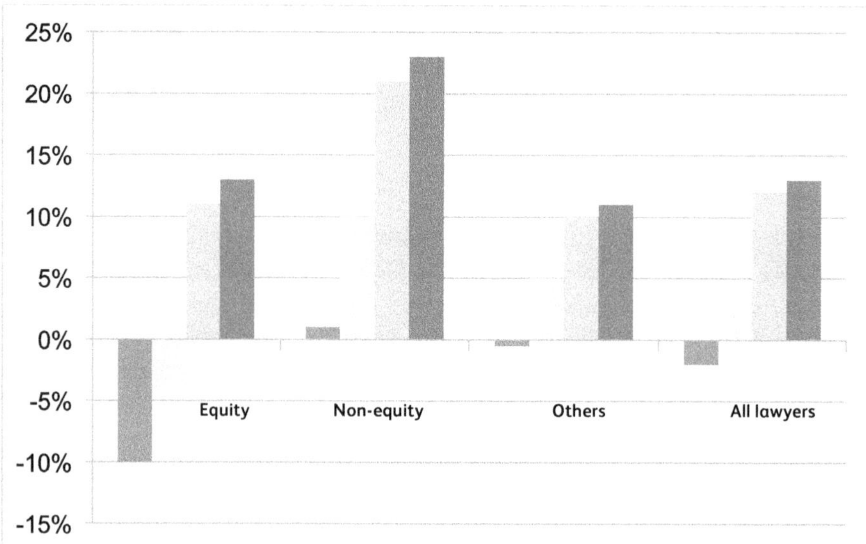

Key: From l-r - 1997; 2001–2010; 2012; 2017

Figure 3

Figure 3 depicts a 20-year look at the rate at which each class of lawyer is over employed – too many lawyers for the volume of work – using the aforementioned productivity levels. For example, in 2017 the AmLaw 200 had more lawyers than it needed for the available work (far right bar, positive 13 percent). Conversely, in 1997 there was more work per lawyer (higher average hours) and the lawyers were exceeding the billable hour targets (left hand bar, negative two percent).

Some recent improvements have occurred, but there may be generational shifts at work as well as fundamental economic forces. Generational shifts are the work/life balance differences from one generation to another. Firms should address this challenge, as the cost of this underproductivity is typically an upper five to low six figure hit to each partner's compensation. For more information, please see the author's webinar on *Too Many Lawyers, Not Enough Work.*[2]

Variables affecting realization

Now let's discuss the variables affecting collected fees. The first variable is the propensity to discount price, which has increased both in the frequency of occurrence and the amount of the discount provided. It is the most common pricing adjustment requested by clients. The second variable is the efficiency at delivering services. Much discussion is underway in the profession about legal project management to improve efficiency and the write-downs that occur before billing due to the lack of efficiency. And those efficiency issues (even with partner-initiated adjustments) carry over to client perceptions of value and the write-offs of accounts receivable after billing. The third variable is how long it takes to bill a client. The fourth variable is how long it takes the client to pay. These last two affect how quickly effort is converted into cash, which affects both profitability and working capital. Slower billing and payment results in statistically less cash ultimately collected and a longer time period for the firm to cover its costs out of working capital.

The illustration that follows depicts what happens at each stage of the fee collection process, beginning with the actual time worked versus the time recorded. This is an elusive metric as it represents individual timekeeper decisions regarding what is and is not appropriate to record. Some of this reflects admonitions from supervising partners, some arises from unease at showing inefficiency, and some is the result of poor time capture habits. Yet, it is an important metric to understand and manage.

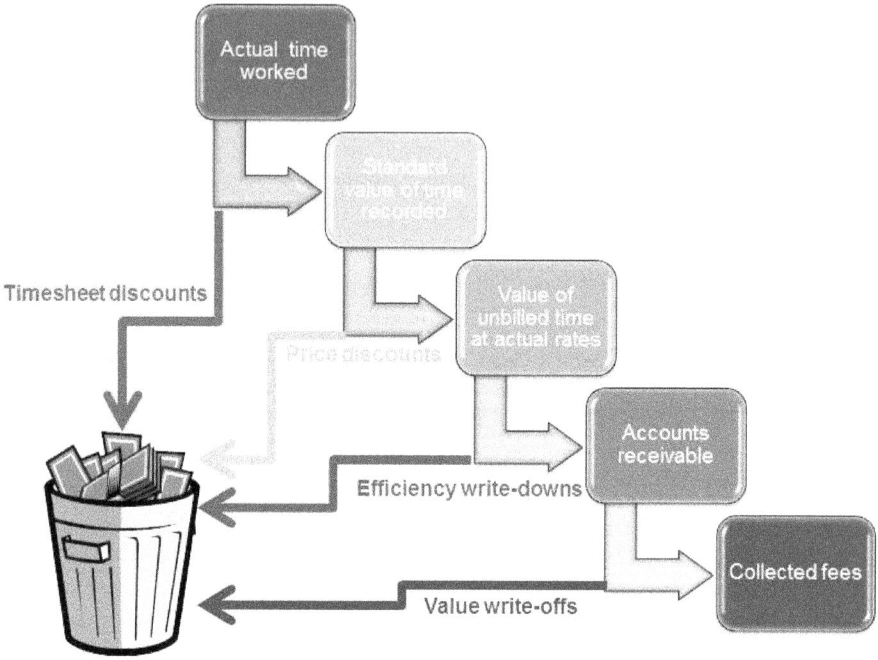

Figure 4

Revenue leakage

Next, we look at the individual components of a common profitability metric – realization. By considering each component separately, we can better understand the problems and correct them (Figure 4). We begin with the standard value of time recorded and the discounts granted to yield the value of time recorded at actual rates. The discounts represent pricing variances.

The firm's unbilled time reports will reflect these actual rate amounts. The relief of unbilled time sends billed time into accounts receivable and billing adjustments for inefficiencies, staffing decisions and the like to the trash. This reduction represents efficiency variances.

Accounts receivable is relieved when cash is collected or accounts are written-off. The write-offs represent collection variances.

Developing a detailed revenue statement

Let us convert this conceptual framework into the following sample revenue statement. The data is from the financial system. The revenue statement begins with standard value of time for the hours recorded and

Revenue	Total	Equity	Non-equity	Associates	Paralegals
Number of timekeepers	5.0	1.0	0.5	2.5	1.0
Hours	500	50	100	250	100
Standard rate	$298	$485	$420	$255	$190
Standard value of time	$149,000	$24,250	$42,000	$63,750	$19,000
Pricing variance (discounts)	-5.0%	-5.0%	-5.0%	-5.0%	-5.0%
Actual rates used	$283	$461	$399	$242	$181
Pricing realization	95.0%	95.0%	95.0%	95.0%	95.0%
Time value at actual rates	$141,550	$23,038	$39,900	$60,563	$18,050
Efficiency adjustments	($11,307)	($691)	($2,394)	($6,056)	($2,166)
Billing realization of actual rates	92.0%	97.0%	94.00%	90.00%	88.00%
Billings	$130,243	$22,346	$37,506	$54,506	$15,884
AR write-offs	($5,210)	($894)	($1,500)	($2,180)	($635)
Collection realization of billings	96.0%	96.0%	96.0%	96.0%	96.0%
Fee collections	$125,033	$21,453	$36,006	$52,326	$15,249
Overall realization of standard rates	83.9%	88.5%	85.7%	82.1%	80.3%

Figure 5

Time value at actual rates	$141,550
Cost of capital (Aaa corporate bond rate)	4.38%
Weeks carried before billing	7
Carrying costs of WIP	**$775**
Billings	$130,243
Cost of capital (Aaa corporate bond rate)	4.38%
Weeks carried before collection	13
Carrying costs of AR	**$1,426**
Total carrying costs	**$2,201**

Figure 6

proceeds as above. However, in this format the financial impact at each stage is evident (Figure 5).

Remember that the cost rates developed earlier in the chapter are based on expected billable time recorded. Thus, the best match of expenses to revenues is to let the cost rates flow from recorded billable hours.

Providing for the speed of billing and collection

We previously mentioned the timeliness of billing and collection efforts as important, yet often un-accounted for factors in assessing profitability. The speed at which billable time is converted into a bill and the bill is paid affects the working capital requirements for the firm. Firms may borrow the funds to carry this investment, resulting in ongoing interest payments. Alternatively, the partners can invest additional capital to carry this burden, for which they should be compensated. All capital comes with a cost for its use. In Figure 6, we used the AAA corporate bond rate as a proxy for the cost of capital. Firms may use their line of credit rate, their bank's prime rate, or some other relevant rate.

Pulling it all together

Now, let us summarize all of this information in Figure 7. It is important to return to the beginning and remember that these efforts are designed to provide reasonable information upon which better decisions can be reached regarding how the firm prices, manages, and delivers legal services. This also provides greater accountability for how well each partner manages his/her practice. This information is not absolute, nor is it without some distortion. However, it does provide a solid foundation.

Revenue	
Standard value	$149,000
Pricing variance (discounts)	($7,450)
Efficiency adjustments	($11,307)
AR write-offs	($5,210)
Net revenue	$125,033
Allocated Expenses	
Compensation and overhead	$100,482
Carrying costs	$2,201
Total costs	$102,683
Contribution	$22,350
Contribution margin	15%

Figure 7

Reference

1. Let us set aside fixed assets and depreciation, clients costs that are supposed to be capitalized, bank borrowings, debt repayment, capital contributions, the return of capital, the year-end pension accrual that is paid in the following year and other minor distortions of pure cash basis accounting.
2. www.altmanweil.com/toomanylawyers.

Chapter 3:
Measure of success – revenue is the ugly cousin of profitability

By Eugenia Frenzel, director of pricing and practice management economics, Perkins Coie

Law firms have been reporting on their revenue for a very long time. Growing up in the legal industry, specifically in big law, revenue measure has been the backdrop that from time to time has been in the spotlight but remained an omnipresent fixture. Ranking tables evolved as a measuring guide to help report on the health and stability of a law firm. Publication of the top ranked 100 and 200 law firms by *American Lawyer* is a highly anticipated event each year. Moving up or down those lists sets off a flurry of speculative reporting as to the reasons a law firm is now in the top 25, 50, 100, or 200 on that list.

Behind the scenes, finance departments within law firms work around the clock to deliver metrics in a timely enough fashion to be included these rankings – regardless of whether internally their fiscal year matches the calendar year. The law firm finance function used to have peak seasons – around the month-end to get bills out the door in a timely manner; calendar year-end to collect before clients close out their annual budgets. That is no longer the case. Billing and collections are a year-round, intense activity, driven by client requirements to deliver timely invoices on the one hand and internal law firm pressures to meet budget goals on the other.

This tracking of law firm revenue creates an air of exclusivity, belonging to a select few that can claim increases year over year. Only a few years ago, law firms were breaking the billion dollar barrier, celebrating achieving their "billion dollar club" status. Now that accomplishment has begun to fade into the past with firms breaking the two and three billion dollar marks.

Much like achieving supersonic speeds in the pursuit of scientific advancement and then keeping our speed limits hovering around 60 miles per hour, it remains to be seen whether chasing the revenue target is a beacon necessary for a law firm's success. It certainly makes for an eye-catching headline. On a more cautionary note, highlighting revenue gains takes attention away from the true test; whether or not that revenue is profitable.

Law firms that do not surface profitability to their partners are in danger of missing the point and perpetuating behaviors that chip away at the bottom line. Let's be clear here. It is hard to argue with revenue, especially with revenue that seems to be increasing year over year. This shifts priorities and possibly misguides credit. It therefore may come as a surprise to learn that many law firms in the top 100, as well as the top 200, are not focused on measuring profitability.

In order to move the needle on profitability, there needs to be adoption. Adoption has been the biggest challenge. Next is transparency. Once there is agreement that a law firm should measure profitability, to what extent that will be visible across the firm quickly becomes the next frontier. None of the effort to adopt and surface profitability is worth a penny unless there are levers to help improve or keep profitability steady.

Take a step back in order to make two steps forward

Adoption of profitability measures in law firms has probably been the biggest hurdle. Adoption requires a shift in culture and, as has been said by many wiser folks, culture in a law firm is its anchor. It is the number one factor that attracts talent to a law firm, it is what retains talent, and it is something that every lawyer and professional staff guards dearly.

The challenge of a culture change to measure the profitability of a law firm is deeply rooted in the history of the legal profession and codified in its ethical code. Lawyers are logical creatures – embracing profitability most often has a negative connotation and signals that somehow the act of minding profit is somehow unethical. Minding profits signals that one is doing something for financial gain. Well, of course, you would say.

Is that not why we are all seeking gainful employment? Empathy and desire to help others are what initially draws people to the legal profession. When you help those who cannot help themselves, when you succeed on behalf of those who have been wronged, when you achieve a resolution that sets the norm for the rest of us – well, that is what brings ultimate satisfaction. Becoming a trusted advisor, stepping in in time of crisis, getting a favorable result, are all building blocks of a lawyer's reputation. To then turn around and admit that those lofty aspirations are after all just a business goes against the very fabric of what makes a lawyer.

Following this thread, that holds true in the context of lawyers providing service to those in need. The logical bridge here is that by providing legal services to those in need for financial gain makes one unethical. After all, lawyers are governed by a code of ethics or – in the modern vernacular – a code of professional standards. Thus, minding profitability is unethical, unethical is a bad word by definition – most recently synonymous with immoral, amoral, unprincipled, unscrupulous, dishonorable, wrong, dishonest, deceitful, disreputable, unconscionable, fraudulent, dirty, unfair, underhand, devious, slippery, bad, wicked, evil, sinful, iniquitous, corrupt, depraved, villainous... and that is just Google's take on it. At least half of those words describe crimes punishable by law. Pause here for a moment. For the master of wordsmithing – if that is a word – that association comes automatically.

What is often missing from the apparently logical stretch between profitability and being ethical is that most often no one is directly impacted by lawyers being compensated for rendering legal services. As my family of doctors often remind me, no one is dying. Unless they are, of course. On death row. Can anyone point to the last time a lawyer represented a death row client for compensation? The irony here is that the legal system has created ways for those who are in real danger of losing their life, or freedom, to receive the necessary legal defense free of charge. When the lawyers in question here – partners in big law – do engage in such honorable work, they do it pro bono.

Society had no need for lawyers until there were certain complexities introduced to the order in our lives. There was no need to have a lawyer when there were no basic human rights. It follows then that the first lawyers were concerned with the matters of individual freedom. Next came property rights. Everything else is an outgrowth of those two basic concepts.

It thus becomes painfully evident that most of the legal work performed today is not of the critical nature of life, freedom, and property. Most of the legal work done today is of the routine, garden variety, business related, in some shape or form. Here is where the idealistic notions of jurisprudence begin to collide with the brute force of business.

Nature versus nurture – it's only nature if it wasn't nurture

It starts in law schools. The grueling curriculum requires a rewiring of the brain that is scary and rewarding at the same time. I will go further and put it out there that, to survive law school, one must possess a masochistic streak. Whether they will admit it to themselves or not, law school graduates have been permanently rewired. Their brain no longer operates like other brains do. This is also where our eager scholars get seriously financially invested. After college, and for many of them after graduate school, newly minted lawyers graduate with several hundreds of thousand dollars of debt.

Being a lawyer is extremely stressful. There is a growing commentary coming forth regarding lawyer mental health. At a recent conference of law firm management, a big chunk of time was devoted to lawyer substance abuse. Whether a law firm is big, mid, or solo, demands are ever growing. What do lawyers get all worked up about? From the time they are young, hungry associates to the days when they are polished partners, the worry is always there – making the filing deadline; knowing their stuff in court in front of the judge, the jury, and fellow counsel; leading a smooth negotiation in front of their client. The level of responsibility is immense, towering, and can be crippling.

How do you then surface focus on increased profitability without sacrificing any actual, or perceived, standards of professional ethics? Moving profitability closer to center stage will reveal a paradigm shift and highlight the next challenge facing business operations in law firms.

Even when profitability is fully embraced at a law firm, lawyers tend to naturally, and often purposefully, gravitate toward lower net profit margins. One way to address this is by including a measure of profitability into the compensation structure. The compensation methodology is an art and a science for which each law firm has its own recipe – from orbiting the opposite moons, to touching lightly, to having a prominent place at the core. Polling law firms may reveal that the exact formula is not the best measure. There is something more fundamental at play.

This reminds me of one of my favorite Aesop's fables about the turtle and the scorpion. It goes something like this:

The scorpion asks the turtle to ferry him across the river and the turtle says: "What if you sting me while we are crossing?" The scorpion laughs out loud and says: "Why would I do that? If I do that we will both drown!" The turtle agrees and lets the scorpion ride on its back. At the midway point, the scorpion stings the turtle. The venom spreads, paralyzing the turtle's every limb and they begin to sink. With its dying breath, the turtle turns her head and asks the scorpion why he did it. "It's in my nature," said the scorpion.

Though not venomous, it can be said that it is the partners' nature to resort to the lowest denominator – to give and promise the lowest rate or the biggest discount.

To illustrate this phenomenon, a conversation with a partner comes to mind. The partner called to ask for forgiveness for, yes, you guessed it. He said that we did not get the work, the client said that our rates were just too high. Sound familiar? The client said the firm they ultimately went with was basically giving them a discount that would amount to a 45 percent discount off this partner's rate. "And you know what I said?" Come on, you know how it goes, right? This is the argument we hear all the time. As the partner was telling me about this client's comments, I pulled up his cost rate. I bet you guessed it already. This is when the partner says, "So I told them that I would match that rate." This partner's cost rate was higher than the billing rate they just agreed to give the client.

But there is more. This client was very thankful and said that if there is any work that the winning law firm would be conflicted out from, or if there is some other overflow, or a referral, the client would come to him. A referral! I gasped. "And I know that it will affect my compensation, but I am willing to take the hit." Yes. There it is. He was willing to take the hit.

But are others willing to do the same? This was an existing client with existing matters that were billed with a discount but not a discount that just he committed to; not only himself but all other attorneys that had open and active matters for this client. He said he spoke with them and they are cool with that. Are they? Did he go on and tell them that they are going to take a hit on their compensation as well? Not sure the conversation went that far. He went on to say that this type of client operates in a small circle and those clients talk and the word will get around that we promised such rates and work is sure to come pouring our way. It is hard to admit, but sometimes "losses" are better "wins".

The issue with adoption and changing behaviors – ultimately making a shift in law firm culture – will need to be addressed at its core, in law schools. It will become imperative to train the lawyers of tomorrow with the skills necessary to be able to navigate the complexities of the legal profession of tomorrow and beyond. Very little is being done at the present in that regard. The number of law schools that are making the business of law and practice management as part of their required curriculum can be counted on one hand. New lawyers will need to have skills, in addition to the solid foundation in jurisprudence, that could meet the rigorous requirements of overseeing and running a multi-million- or billion-dollar enterprise.

It should be noted, that the focus here is on the profitability of legal work, whether at a matter or client level, not individual fee earner profitability. An important distinction that may be overlooked. When looking at matter profitability, there are concrete levers that can be used to move the needle. There are efficiencies that can be found, processes improved, and staffing optimized. Individual profitability tends to cross into realm of talent management and that is out of scope of this discussion.

It is a very interesting time in law firms right now. There are a good number of firms that are looking at profitability, all with a varying degree of transparency. Of profitability metrics surfacing to the select few in the partnership to the whole partnership. Focus on revenue, however, tends to cultivate the type of incentives that go against the grain of a partnership fabric. Brash and swift deals begin to take hold without regard to the bottom line. It behooves me to propose that a focus on profitability is what is needed to preserve the elegance of the train of thought of the legal profession in an age of rapid change, inevitability of standardization of legal work, and the tsunami of data.

Chapter 4:
Avoiding false profits – a guide

By Timothy B Corcoran, principal at Corcoran Consulting Group LLC

For a business to be sustainable in the long run, particularly when facing competitive threats and constant market disruptions, its leaders must first understand the drivers of business success and then take corrective action when the drivers and the results no longer produce the desired outcome. While it's refreshing to see progress, it's also a bit disconcerting that so many law firm leaders are just now beginning to ask questions about how to measure profitability. Of course, what's even more astounding is the number of law firm leaders who resolutely *aren't* trying to develop a more precise understanding of what drives profits in their firms. "We're profitable and that's that," they say. "If we dig too deeply, we risk damaging our collegial culture." And thus they blithely march on, idolizing the "classic" measures of high billing rates and profits per partner as proxies for actual insight.

But judgement day is nigh, and those idolizing false profits will soon feel the wrath of an angry deity who… wait, no. They won't feel anything. There's no such day of reckoning. In reality, a ruthless market will simply and increasingly ignore law firms whose leaders' pursuit of outdated success metrics position them loudly and wildly out of sync with market demand. So how does a modern law firm leader avoid this fate? Let's start by examining the traditional approaches to measuring profitability in a law firm. And then let's examine how ineffective these measures can be in today's market. Finally, we'll examine the next two frontiers in law firm profitability – the voice of the client and time.

Do your dishes

For many lawyers, an open discussion of the pursuit of profit can appear unseemly. Of course, there is potentially significant value in providing competent legal counsel to those in need, such as to a small business owner in a contract dispute, or to a multinational corporation in the midst of a merger, or to an individual purchasing a new home. Many lawyers have considered profit to be an inevitable byproduct of successfully managing a case or a file, and not itself the objective. The only thing worth talking about is how to deliver quality legal work, not the messy business of profits. However, today's law firm leaders are learning that pursuing profit, let alone discussing it, isn't unseemly. Rather, it's a key way to ensure that the firm is providing quality legal services, at competitive market prices, to price-conscious buyers, and generating sufficient value to reward the lawyers engaged in the practice of law.

Yet some leaders still proceed too slowly in the development of a culture based on profitability rather than on production. It can be political suicide in firms with significant disparity in partner billing rates. High billing rate partners may advocate for profit calculations based on an oft-misguided view that high rates equal high profits, and they want to be paid more. Lower billing rate partners, or older partners whose receivables are dwarfed by their current compensation, will vigorously reject more nuanced profit calculations, lest their compensation take a hit. They'll claim that the firm's family culture will suffer if partners are singled out for performance issues.

I don't know about your family, but in my family on Thursday evenings when it was time for my older brother to clear the table and load the dishwasher, if he flatly refused we didn't roll our eyes and chuckle indulgently and then do it for him out of respect for family harmony. We expected him to pull his weight. But we didn't have similar expectations for how my infant sister should contribute. Families hold each other accountable, but accountability doesn't have to be the same for all. Think of profit calculations as a way to measure whether partners are meeting expectations. It's perfectly acceptable to have different expectations based on skillsets and opportunities. Everyone has to do their dishes.

Redefining profit

The traditional unsophisticated approach to measuring profit involves adding total cash receipts received during the fiscal year and then subtracting the annual costs to operate the firm. What remains is profit, and this is distributed in total to the equity partners, and the process repeats the following year. This aggregate approach tends to mask under-performance, but it also masks over-performance. It's more than likely that the firm delivers some legal services at a significant loss, but so long as other services deliver a significant premium, no one's the wiser. This is why PPP or profits per partner is such an opaque metric for assessing the fiscal health of a law firm, or for comparing two law firms. The underlying performance is wholly unknown when everything is rolled up.

In a competitive marketplace, the best way to sustain a competitive advantage is to know explicitly and then to pursue those services that can be delivered profitably. It's also helpful to set prices and allocate resources based on an understanding of the underlying profit contributions of different practices, industries, offices, and matter types. No, this doesn't automatically mean that the most profitable work should receive the most resources – in fact, mathematically speaking, doing so would quickly impair profitability – but it means that firm leaders will better know where to allocate resources in order to boost or maintain profits. Done effectively, a low rate but high-volume practice that some would starve of resources might benefit greatly from an investment in practice re-engineering, potentially delivering substantial profits, albeit at low margins. Matters with declining margins due to price pressure might benefit from different staffing approaches. Matters with already high profits might earn a price *increase*, if analysis reveals high unmet market demand. In most law firms, different matters and even different practices operate across a spectrum of profitability, meaning one-size-fits-all management solutions fit none.

To properly calculate profit, we must make a number of choices. The first is the level at which profit will be measured. Aggregate organizational profit is a blunt instrument and wholly unhelpful to guide management decisions. It's more useful to understand the profitability of a timekeeper and a matter. If we understand these, we can also calculate the profitability of a client, a practice, an office, or an industry.

Assumption consumption

There are a number of assumptions embedded in the analysis of timekeeper and matter profitability, and it cannot be overstated how critical they are to influencing and/or understanding the result. In most cases, there isn't a clear right or wrong approach, but in the absence of a common understanding, the mismatched expectations will lead to unrest and unnecessary strife.

Cash vs accrual

Law firms rely on a "cash is king" approach and therefore only record revenues received and expenses incurred within a given fiscal time period. So a lawyer with time billed in one year is considered unprofitable if invoices aren't paid until the next year. And a lawyer paid a contingency fee this year but who booked all hours on the matter in prior years is considered extraordinarily profitable. When we jumble together all costs and all receivables for all matters in a given year, we hope that these variations wash out. But that's like dropping a new and vividly red bath towel into your washing machine with your whites and colors and accepting that from now on every outfit you wear is slightly pink. Other businesses generally rely on an accrual accounting approach that links the costs and revenues together, irrespective of timing. This approach potentially provides more accurate insights into matter and timekeeper profitability, which in turn can help guide staffing and pricing decisions.

Overhead allocations

Many firms burden matter and timekeeper profitability with the costs of operating the business. Every timekeeper is allocated some pro rata share of indirect expenses such as rent, healthcare, staff salaries, etc., whether or not the timekeeper utilizes these services in a pro rata fashion. Inevitably this leads to amusing arguments: "I only used 1/8th of an accounting clerk's time last month because my time entries are written legibly, so I shouldn't have to pay full price for the accounting team," and "The real estate group's square footage within our offices is 40 percent smaller than litigation, so we shouldn't have to bear an equal share of the lease."

Regardless of the validity of these arguments, so long as these costs are allocated equitably and consistently, the profit calculations aren't usually all that sensitive to minor tweaks. However, we could argue that accounting profit, or what we capture for financial reporting purposes, is very different to matter profitability calculations, which can guide battlefield decisions on staffing and pricing. An alternative is to ignore indirect expense allocations (consider them a firm expense stewarded by the firm's elected leaders) and focus solely on direct expenses, e.g., timekeepers, technology, and disbursements, that are specifically linked to a specific matter.

Utilization

A common approach to timekeeper profitability spreads direct and indirect costs across the timekeeper's worked hours, so simple math means those who work more hours will have a lower cost per hour. As a result, partners who are monitoring profitability are pushed toward using highly-utilized associates and treating under-utilized associates as if they carry a contagious disease. The rich get richer. While this may appear sensible on paper, in reality partners must grasp that carrying the costs of idle associates – their salaries, benefits, office space, etc., – can quickly erode profits gained elsewhere. Another approach is to incorporate "standard" or target hours into timekeeper and matter profitability for the purposes of pricing and staffing, and rely on actual hours for assessing productivity.

Managers and rainmakers

For timekeepers who primarily bill hours, it's fairly straightforward to deduct their costs from the revenue resulting from their billed hours. Lawyers serving in management roles and rainmakers pose a different challenge, as they tend to have fewer billed hours. The net result is their profitability appears low. A misguided but astonishingly common response, therefore, is for rainmakers to stop selling new work and go back to the office and bill time, and for managers to neglect their supervisory duties to tend to their own book of business. It should come as no surprise that practice group leaders responsible for doling out work occasionally dole out work to themselves in order to keep pace. An alternative is to establish a standard cost "plug" that can be applied to those engaged primarily in other activities, though of course these other activities must be deemed valuable to the firm and those treated as such must be accountable to engaging in these activities.

Pricing for profit

The combination of these and related assumptions will produce different results, so it's important to understand the business purposes for which each calculation is most helpful. As firm information systems grow in sophistication, it's common for leaders to be presented with different dashboards depending on business purpose. Profit can be influenced and measured at multiple stages of the legal services delivery process, so it's important to provide analysis and decision support information in a way that's easily understood and digestible for the intended audience.

A key opportunity precipitated by a deeper understanding of profit is to be more strategic in pricing legal services. Traditionally, law firm pricing has been set from the inside out, or setting a price that covers the law firm's expenses and generates a healthy profit, often independent of what the market might be willing to pay. As clients have flexed their buying muscles, law firms have had to embrace what every other business segment long ago realized – value is defined by the buyer. When a sophisticated buyer of legal services knows he can buy at half price and at greater quality that which he once purchased from a traditional law firm, the end game for the law firm is either obsolescence or adaptation. But when adapting means lowering prices to meet market realities, this doesn't have to mean lower profits and smaller distributions for partners. By understanding what drives profitability, lawyers can re-engineer the work to make money even when revenue is flat or declining.

Law firm leaders must link pricing to profitability. Rather than maximizing hours, or even rate, the goal is to maximize profit. There are numerous levers available for partners to boost matter profitability, including staffing, technology, and automation. Similarly, there are numerous ways to boost firm profitability, including high utilization, high realization, client retention, and client penetration (aka cross selling). The critical adjustment to the art of pricing is *knowing what the market is willing to pay for a service*. Without this knowledge, it's sheer luck when the price charged is roughly equivalent to the client's perceived value.

It's not uncommon to hear a smug senior partner boast, "My rates have never been challenged by a client". It's also increasingly common for a sheepish partner to lament, "My client apparently doesn't care about quality; they just want lower rates". What these both have in common is a lack of understanding of market value. When a client has never complained about a price, it usually means the product is under-priced for the value delivered. When a client fixates solely on price, it usually means the product is over-priced for the value delivered. As we incorporate profitability metrics, we can shift away from a goal of selling as many hours as possible at the highest rates possible to a goal of maximizing profits, even if this means raising or lowering the price, or spending more or less time delivering the work.

Rewarding profit, not production

A discussion of profitability is interesting but futile if the partners don't act accordingly to change their behavior. In many law firms, there's a clear recognition of the importance of profits over hours, but there's no incentive to change focus. Partners continue to make choices that, unfortunately, pit the firm's long-term financial interests against their individual interests. It doesn't have to be that way. Managing partners often exhort their partners to act in a "firm first" manner, which is an acknowledgement that the partners have a choice. Instead of offering a choice of acting for or against the firm's interests, the choice for partners should be between maximizing one's compensation by furthering the firm's interests or limiting one's compensation by acting selfishly. The culture might not allow de-equitization or ousting a partner who refuses to collaborate, but the compensation plan can certainly withhold rewards for those who take more from the firm than they give. It's the responsibility of management to align what's good for the partner with what's good for the firm. Asking partners to find and then pursue this path on their own is simply poor management.

It's also important to note that not all partners are motivated by financial rewards. An effective compensation plan also serves as a guiding principle for what it means to be an owner of the firm and it helps to manage expectations by linking rewards with actions. Modernizing a partner compensation plan can be time-consuming and cumbersome, and even when there's a clear vision of the desired end state it might take a few years to implement because of the risk of disruption. Nevertheless, it's critical to incorporate measures of profit in partner compensation.

The most critical aspect of a partner compensation plan, and a goal that must be maintained throughout any adjustments to formulae, processes, or dashboards, is transparency. Whether the plan is formulaic or subjective, open or closed, driven by an elected committee or by senior management, the most important goal is for the plan to provide clear guidance to partners as to what rewards will ensue when they engage in certain behaviors. The goal is not merely to reward profitable behavior, but to *drive* it.

This is not a task for the faint-hearted, which is why so many law firm leaders avoid it. However, anything less just "kicks the can down the road" to the next management regime.

Building a profit culture

Given law firms' longstanding focus on measures of production, it may take some time to build momentum to adopt measures of profitability. It's important to move thoughtfully and in stages in order to avoid significant disruption. These stages draw on the experience of fellow contributor Madhav Srinivisan and other financial professionals who have been down this road.

Measure

Firm leaders work through a variety of approaches for measuring profit, sometimes behind the scenes. While it's helpful to have a mandate from the partners, it's not necessary. Once a suitable model is ready, it's important to embrace change management principles to gain buy-in. Avoid "revealing" profit policies to partners with no warning, or risk revolt.

Monitor

Once established, the profit measures are incorporated into the firm's financial systems, with reports in selected and targeted areas issued periodically. Management also provides targeted education to help partners understand how to incorporate profit measures into battlefield decisions.

Manage

As profit measures become more ingrained, management shifts to sharing deeper insights into the underlying drivers of profitability and providing training to help partners make better decisions. Management targets specific matters, clients, and timekeepers for additional support to improve performance.

Master

At this stage, all partners have had intensive training and are expected to know and incorporate measures of profit into their decisions, e.g., pricing, staffing, etc. Where partners fall short, corrective action is taken. There is no opt out.

Motivate

Some partners will change behavior only when there are economic benefits or consequences in the compensation plan. For those not motivated solely by financial considerations, the compensation plan linked to the annual business planning process can serve as an excellent roadmap for incorporating more profitable actions.

The future of profitability

An unfortunate consequence of law firms' adherence to cash-based accounting principles is how it pushes partners to think of all outlays as costs to be minimized or avoided. Should we agree to sponsor this client event? Only if we think we'll get some business from it. Should we open a new office? Only if it can pay for itself right away. Should we hire this lateral partner? Only if she brings a large book of business. This mindset forces short-term thinking. In most businesses, we take a longer-term view. Some outlays are one-time costs, never to be recovered, and these should be minimized. Other outlays, however, pay a significant return, though that return may materialize only after a period of loss.

In the current climate, a law firm partner is recognized and rewarded for pursuing actions that maximize billable hours and revenue right now, even if this creates client dissatisfaction. The alternative is to bend to the client's will, such as by accepting a non-hourly fee or negotiating lower rates, and accept punishment in the form of a lower profit rating or lower compensation. But imagine a world in which partners' interests were aligned with the clients', and investments in more strategic pricing, better staffing, technology automation, process improvement and project management, and cross-selling were rewarded both by the client and by firm management. This is where the future of profitability takes us. Simply put, if we measure profitability on a one-year basis, we'll encourage short-term decisions that have long-term consequences. If we measure profitability over a longer time period, we foster an environment in which maximizing profits means securing repeat engagements, and this in turn only comes from delighting clients.

Just as a business might establish a multi-year business case for investing in new equipment for the factory floor, offsetting the initial purchase price with increased revenues from higher capacity production runs that require less manpower to operate, a law firm can do the same. What we're looking for is the profits that ensue from a client hiring the firm again and again, across a variety of practices, and committing to certain price points for work that has value, without meddling in how the firm produces the work product. This is where profitability is the real driver of growth. The two key ingredients are time and client input.

Clients have developed a stronger understanding of the value ascribed to certain legal services and they're signaling and even outright declaring their budgets. It's time to listen. Rather than reject calls for alternative pricing or for discounts, seek to understand why the client perceives this work to have declining value. Work with the client to re-engineer the work to meet their quality standards while also generating short-term profits – even at a lower price point. Limit the number of "loss leader" matters partners pursue in the hope of securing more lucrative work down the road. Work to make all matters profitable. In return, ask clients to commit to the firm, and many will. This same rigor will also identify work that clients highly value and that deserves a premium price.

In the journey towards adopting a more modern sense of law firm profitability, there will be a number of roadblocks, detours, diversions, and shiny things to capture your attention. Don't be dazzled by technology tools, or be crippled by recalcitrant partners, or be awed by complexity. As with all successful journeys, it starts with a few simple steps in the right direction. We can't go backward, but we can learn the way from those who have made this trek before us. It's time to get started.

Chapter 5:
A roadmap to effective profitability reporting

By Peter Lane Secor, chief pricing officer, Pepper Hamilton LLP

This chapter will help you manage your profit reporting, assist in gaining acceptance of client/matter profitability, and ultimately improve performance. The most important things to remember are:

- If there are no revenues, you have a bigger problem than profitability;
- It takes time to improve profitability – there is no magic switch; and
- There is always a story, and that's okay.

A partner once said that analyzing law firm profit is relative – relative to market, resources, and demand. Of course, they were right. I view profitability as a guide. There is no right or wrong answer. For example, when using a fully loaded profit methodology, breakeven is not a zero net margin – it is plus or minus five percent. This is true regardless of the profit methodology being used.

So, what are the tips and tricks of effective profitability reporting? Since profitability holds people accountable, it is extremely important that the information is accurate and timely. Nothing will disrupt profit reporting more than having inaccurate information or calculations. Because profit data comes from more than one source, it can be tricky. Some of the data elements include FTEs (full time equivalencies), salaries, and partner compensation. If any of these data points or other calculations, such as overhead allocations, are not correct, then the armor of profit reporting is pierced.

Bottom line – if data calculations are wrong, profit will be dismissed. To make sure our numbers are correct, we tie out to our cash-based income statement every month, even though our primary profit reporting is on an accrual basis. Accurate reporting is a great way to gain acceptance.

Then let people see the numbers and ask the tough questions. Do not try to shove the results down someone's throat, especially attorneys who want to understand profitability and, hopefully, how best to use it. Give them what they want to see.

Providing various ways to view profit is a successful strategy. There are many ways to calculate and report on profit. For example, you may have folks who want to look only at direct margin, fully-loaded net margin using standard costing, fully-loaded net margin using actual costing, net margin without partner compensation, cash vs accrual, and more. Do not be afraid to provide various versions of profit. It can even all be done in one profit statement. If a particular margin or method gets buy-in, incorporate that into your reporting. The goal is to help people understand and use profit as a guide or tool. Most people do not subscribe to showing profit in multiple ways, i.e., a "pick one and go with it" approach. The problem is that forcing one method often causes resentment, making people shy away from using the tool.

A sample profit statement

Opposite is an example of a profit statement with multiple KPIs (key performance indicators) – effective realization, actual billing realization, direct margin, net margin (in two flavors), contribution without partner compensation and more.

This profit statement/report uses both standard and actual costing. Standard costing uses a standard number of units – in this case, hours to assign the cost for each hour. For example, we might assign partners 1,600 hours and associates 1,900 hours. Their total costs, however defined – just direct costs, compensation or direct costs and indirect costs, overhead – are divided by the standard hours. The value of using standard costing is that profit is not impacted by how busy timekeepers are, so it is an excellent method to understand how well an engagement is priced. Standard costing is not impacted by volume fluctuations. It provides a lens as if everyone worked the same number of hours. Of course, in reality this just doesn't happen. By using the constant of standard hours, the resulting margins (direct or net) are true and accurate indications of the profitability of a fee/arrangement.

The last section reports contribution without partner compensation. It shows partner earnings, profit without consideration of what partners are compensated, i.e., what partners earned after paying for everything else. By dividing the partner FTE, we get PPP (profit per partner). Even more importantly, we can calculate the PPPH (profit per partner hour),

Sample statement

Sample statement	
Standard amount	Standard costing (cost based on standard hours)
Expected amount	
Expected realization %	
Direct costs	
Cost write-downs (WIP)	
Cost write-offs (AR)	
Direct margin	
DM %	
Indirect costs	
Bonuses and comp adjustments	
Standard net margin	
SNM %	
Utilization adjustment	Actual costing (cost based on actual hours)
Utilization Net Margin	
UNM %	
Contribution No Partner Comp	
PPP contribution	
PPPH contribution	

Additional information

- Hours worked
- FTE
- Partner hours
- Attorney non partner hours
- Non partner hours
- Attorney leverage
- Firm leverage
- Bill amount, regardless of work date
- Billing amount % (vs std)
- Collect amount, regardless of work date*
- Unbilled amount of work
- Collected amount of work
- Uncollected amount of work
- Standard rate
- Negotiated/system rate
- Billed rate
- Partner FTE

*Showing the "collected amount, revenue regardless of work date" makes it easy to convert net margin to cash basis.

which is something I learned from the people at Positive Pricing. This is an extremely valuable KPI. It is the lowest common denominator of profit reporting and shows the amount each partner makes for every hour they work. Without a doubt, it is the strongest number of profitability. When you work with a partner on any level of profit reporting – department, practice group, office, client, or matter – and can tell them this is how much you put in your pocket for every hour you work, it gets their attention and they take action.

To provide all this information it is necessary to provide a glossary of terms and calculations.

Glossary of terms and calculations

I. Terminology

A. **Hours worked** – actual hours worked.

B. **Standard amount** – hours multiplied by standard rate.

C. **Expected amount** – expected collections, standard value adjusted for client deal, if applicable and actual billing write-ups (downs). Further adjusted based on the client's historical billing write-ups (downs) and historical receivables write-offs. This amount "matures" over time. It starts out as unbilled, once billed becomes billed, and then once collected becomes the actual collected amount.

D. **Expected %** – expected amount divided by standard amount.

E. **Direct costs** – direct cost associated with production of standard value, the cost of all timekeeper wages, plus X% for taxes/benefits and partner distributions limited to their standard value of work; see Comp adjustment. Budgeted distributions are used for the current year and actual distributions for historical years. Further adjusted for any write-downs or write-offs of any disbursements.

F. **Direct margin** – expected revenue less direct expense, cost write-offs, and cost write-downs.

G. **Direct margin %** – direct margin divided by standard amount.

H. **Indirect cost** – overhead, all other costs not directly associated with the production of revenue; i.e. rent, support staff, all benefits, etc. Allocated by office and then national costs.

I. **Comp adjustment** – all bonuses and partner management *or overhead adjustment, for partner distributions in excess of potential standard value earnable, (amount above XXXX hours multiplied by standard rate).* Essentially an adjustment for highly compensated partners.

J. **Standard net margin** – direct margin less indirect costs and comp adjustment.

K. **Standard net margin %** – standard net margin divided by standard amount.

L. **Utilization adjustment** – the variance between standard direct cost by hour and the actual direct cost by hour multiplied by hours worked.

M. **Utilization (actual) net margin** – standard net margin plus or minus utilization adjustment.

N. **Utilization (actual) net margin %** – utilization net margin divided by standard amount.

II. Net margins

A. Standard net margin:

1. Net margin if everyone worked the same amount of hours.
2. Calculated based on anticipated hours and does not fluctuate based on utilization.
    a. Partners: X,XXX
    b. Associates: X,XXX
    c. Of Counsel: X,XXX
    d. Paralegal: X,XXX
3. Helps understand if the work for the client was priced right/ sustainable.
4. Standard net margin is helpful in understanding client profitability because it does not take into account timekeeper utilization.
    a. Clients are not responsible for how busy people are.

B. Utilization (actual) net margin:

1. Utilization net margin or actual net margin takes into account how busy or slow timekeepers are.
    a. Because compensation is fixed:
        (1) More hours = lower direct cost per hour
        (2) Fewer hours = higher direct cost per hour

How to use this information

With all of these measures in your arsenal, what should you do next? The answer is regular and frequent reporting. Don't let profit become something that is dusted off in Q4 to "see how we are doing". Make it part of monthly reporting to spot trends and be proactive, and work regularly with department/practice group leaders, directors, and executive management. Admittedly, there is not a lot of value reporting on profit the first few months of a year. But do make profit reporting part of the monthly routine. Then once Q1 is complete, step it up and distribute the reporting.

What should you distribute? Don't try to get too granular. It is not necessary to provide initial reporting at the attorney, client, or matter level. Typically, firms report on both the department and practice group levels. If there are issues, and there will be, you can always drill down into the lower levels – working attorneys, billing attorneys, offices, clients, etc.

For me, part of the reporting process is not just generating reports and hitting send. It is analyzing the results. As part of our reporting process, we use overall firm results and budgeted expectations as benchmarks. We also compare the current results to prior months and prior years. These comparisons include realization, direct margin, net margin, leverage, inventories, net margin without partner compensation, rates (standard, negotiated, billed, collected), PPP, and PPPH. It is a lot of information, especially if you multiply it by the number of departments and practice groups in your firm. However, a full analysis is doable and important. Set aside the time to review the results with at least one other person. It then becomes a conversation uncovering "the good, the bad, and the ugly". Have your profit system available so you can do the drill down to find and report on the reasons. It can become a bit of a fishing excursion, but every time you do the review you will get better at it. It takes us just over an hour to review five departments and 15 practice groups. If we find particular issues, they are escalated to the appropriate people to address concerns.

We provide a quarterly written executive analysis of each area, where we focus on the good news and downplay the negatives. As mentioned earlier, there is always a story – a timekeeper who is struggling, a client in a cash flow crunch, an old rate arrangement that hasn't been addressed, and more. I like to read a proxy to get in the mindset. Then I just report the facts with supporting detail. Doing this provides executive management with a cheat sheet of things they might want to focus on.

Unfortunately, even with the best intentions of sharing positive information, most of the time we are forced to point out underperformers, be they whole practice groups, specific billing attorneys, working attorneys, or specific clients. This gets even more difficult when you try to interject potential solutions – fire that client, reduce that person's pay, move the timekeeper to the Chattanooga office or to another practice area.

Beyond straight reporting, it is also important that people have regular access to profit results. Dashboards or reporting tools can help share the information by providing the ability to look at various profit slices, i.e., working attorney, billing attorney, originating attorney, titles, departments, practice groups, geographical regions, clients, matter types, industries, and more. Not only does this let people dive in themselves, but it also builds confidence in the data. When people look at the data closer and see that underlying data is correct, they begin to trust the results and use it make decisions. Profit access becomes even more critical if it is a measure of partner compensation decisions. If you are going to measure people by anything they need to have access to the data so they can manage the results.

But, again I go back to the plus or minus five percent. It is in the ball bark. No major surgery is required, like transitioning out a client, an industry, an area of law, a geographic region, or a practice. Profit reporting is a guide. We aren't going to change on a dime, and need to think long-term. This is where pricing strategies become important. Do we resist a client that provides low margins and high volume? Do we invest in nurturing the relationships, value adds, and "freebies?"

These nuances are constantly changing, creating new opportunities and challenges. Profitability reporting can help position firms, departments, and practice groups to make strategic decisions. Are we willing and able to offer a deep discount to get a certain volume of work? How much do we want to put in our pocket for every hour we work? What changes do we need to make to have the right mix of resources? How do we leverage talent, resources, project management, and technology? Today, more than ever, good lawyers and clients strive for quality and efficiencies. Profitability reporting provides the analytics on the success or failure of business models, but does not provide the qualitative value of legal capabilities lawyers practice in the pursuit of justice. Earnings and profit are simply the results of their sustained effort and success.

Chapter 6:
Tackling partner compensation

By Ron Paquette, director of pricing, Akerman LLP

If you are reading this book, you already know that lawyers (and this industry as a whole) are a distinct group. While many self-identify as weak in math or finances and a good number have not spent any significant time thinking about the business of law, we must recognize their unique training as we approach profitability. Lawyers are trained to absorb large quantities of information and distill it into something more manageable and logical. They are also trained to find seemingly small issues and use them to discredit an entire position – remember Johnnie Cochran's famous line, "If it doesn't fit, you must acquit" from the OJ Simpson trial? This was arguably a single issue that impacted a trial with plenty of other evidence pointing to an alternative conclusion.

In addition to their unique thought process, simply the mention of profitability can have the unintentional effect of instilling fear in the minds of some attorneys, especially those with the most to lose (highest compensation). People don't like to be corrected or have their faults (or opportunities) pointed out to them, least of all if their reputation, standing in the firm, or compensation might be impacted by the conclusions drawn. Because we are dealing with a potentially resistant population with strong critical thinking skills, it is vital that we get profitability modeling right. If it is not right, we risk losing credibility in the model and potentially the team overall.

Partner compensation is the most often overlooked factor in client and matter profitability modeling – most firms have not spent sufficient time thinking about how compensation is handled in their model and the downstream impacts. How much of a partner's total compensation should be allocated to the work he or she performs on a matter and what should be excluded from these analyses? This topic may not be as prevalent as revenue recognition (cash or accrual) or the standard versus actual hours debate, but since it disproportionately impacts the highest compensated partners, it is an essential component to a robust and thorough profitability model. In this chapter, we will explore the various ways that firms have approached partner compensation in client and matter profitability models, along with the associated strengths and weaknesses.

Before we get into the methodologies, let's get a few things out of the way. First, I am assuming that you have the basics of your matter and client profitability model determined already (cash/accrual, standard/actual hours, overhead allocation, etc.). Second, in this chapter, we are exclusively talking about client and matter profitability or margins. Attorney, practice, office and group profitability should be fully loaded and have another methodology and set of assumptions. With a matter and client profitability model, there are two primary goals:

- Inform pricing decisions in the pitch or planning phase; and
- Management and improvement of existing relationships – identify and emulate strong performers; assess and prescribe change for under-performers.

Why does it matter?

Partners impact the firm in a multitude of ways and, for most firms, compensation follows these contributions – working on client files, managing and billing, originating, attorney mentorship, firm management activities, and, of course, firm ownership (Figure 1). Should the compensation from all of these contributions be considered? We could argue at length about the merits of including or excluding each factor, but when we finally come to a mutual agreement, does your firm explicitly break down compensation by contributing factor? In other words, can you say that, of a partner's total compensation, X percent is for their working hours, Y percent is for their billing attorney responsibilities, etc.? Without this categorization of compensation, we are left instead to create a model to accomplish this need. This methodology must be fair to the lawyers, work within the context of your firm's culture, and it must generate the expected conclusions and actions. Allocate too much compensation (or all of it) or too little and this decision could be the sole driving factor for a matter appearing as a performance outlier (significantly above or below the firm average). What are the ways that firms are determining costs for a partner in the context of a matter/client profitability or margin model? This chapter will review the most common (and one or two uncommon) approaches along with the associated risks or issues with each. Unfortunately, a perfect solution has not been found so I cannot make a "one size fits all" recommendation but hopefully there is enough below to guide you in your analysis and decision-making process.

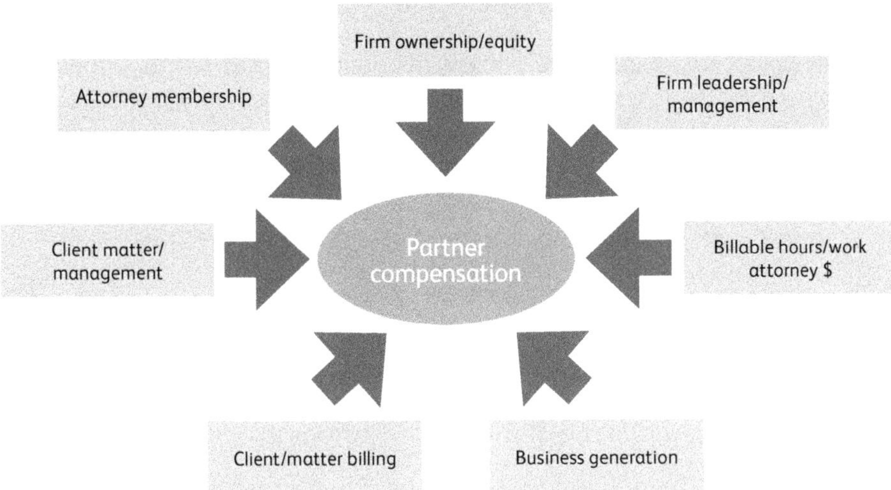

Figure 1: Why does it matter?

Before we go through the methods in detail, let's first look at the extremes – fully loaded (too much), and no partner direct costs (too little). Hopefully, seeing these examples will make it clear why you want to take a more nuanced approach.

Fully loaded

Partner A has over 20 years' experience in a small to mid-market city with a standard billing rate of \$550. However, due to a very large portfolio of work, this partner is compensated \$1.1m per year. All partners in this firm have an expectation of 1,700 billable hours and overhead of \$225k per year. Without any adjustments, this creates a standard cost rate of \$780 per hour, \$230 more than the partner's standard billing rate:

$$\text{Hourly cost rate} = \frac{(\text{Compensation + overhead})}{\text{Standard hours}}$$

$$= \frac{(\$1{,}100{,}000 + \$225{,}000)}{1{,}700} = \$780 \text{ per hour}$$

This partner works on a single matter with a mid-level associate who has a standard billing rate of $400 and a cost rate of $195. Partner A was not involved in originating and is not the billing attorney – his only involvement is through his legal expertise and time billed to the matter. The client was offered a 10 percent discount and paid in full without any write-offs or write-downs. The partner leverages the associate for 65 percent of the billable hours, working the remaining 35 percent. The result of this matter is a margin of just two percent when the firm average is above 20 percent.

	Partner A	Associate	Total
Hours worked	7	13	20
Standard value	$3,850	$5,200	$9,050
Billable value/revenue	$3,465	$4,680	$8,145
Allocated costs	$(5,460)	$(2,535)	$(7,995)
Margin	$(1,995)	$2,145	$150
Margin %	-58%	46%	2%

In this scenario, what prescription would you give to the partner to improve the margins?

There are only a handful of levers available for improvement:

- Discounting? Discounts were limited to 10 percent, below the firm average of 13 percent. Eliminating discounts would still only increase margins to 11 percent.
- Write-offs? No write-offs or write-downs were performed.
- Leverage? The associate worked 1.85 hours for each partner hour. To achieve firm average margins, the partner would need to work less than 18 percent of the time – this may not be feasible.
- Substitution? Could another, lower cost, partner work this time? Possibly. But, is this repeatable to all of this partner's matters?

Ultimately, while there are minor adjustments that could improve the margins on this matter, there are only two conclusions remaining. The first is that Partner A should not perform this work. The second is that extreme leverage combined with full-rates is the only way to have positive margins when working with this partner. Either conclusion will likely create distrust in the profitability model and will ultimately result in a loss of credibility for the model and your team. Your model must find a balance that allows attorneys to build a portfolio of work while still being involved in the execution of client work. Yes, there are likely partners that the firm would like to encourage to spend more time in business development but that is not effectively accomplished by making their existing work look unprofitable. Additionally, it is a very rare partner that has a significant book of business without working any billable hours to support it.

At a firm level, fully loading compensation might look like Figure 2, where we have plotted margin percent at standard rates (1 – cost rate/standard rate) against direct costs (compensation) for each timekeeper. In this chart, you can see that we have several dozen timekeepers with negative margins and another handful with slim margins (less than 10-15 percent) that will become negative with even small discounts. These timekeepers are the ones we are trying to address through this process.

Figure 2: Fully loaded partner costs

No partner direct costs

In this approach, partners only have indirect costs allocated to the clients on which they work. I have not heard of a firm using this model in quite a few years but when it was discussed, this was done for two reasons. The first reason was that the firm desired to keep actual partner compensation out of any reporting in order to support their closed compensation system. The second reason comes from thinking about firm profit and loss (P&L) statements where partner compensation is the distribution of profits and therefore not included in costs. While this approach does achieve those goals, it creates other issues, namely what I call the King Midas Effect – and all partners will have it.

Let's bring back Partner A from above, except now with no direct costs. The cost rate is now just \$132 (\$225,000 in overhead divided by the 1,700 standard hours) – a lower cost rate than the associate. At the standard rates discussed, this creates a margin of 76 percent (1 – cost rate/standard rate) for each hour worked by the partner and 51 percent for the associate. In order for Partner A to have margins as low as the associate, his rate would need to be discounted to \$272 (50 percent discount). Do we really think it is reasonable to assert that a 20-year partner working for \$272 carries the same relative margin as a mid-level associate working at full rates? Keep in mind that this result would be magnified for partners in larger markets where rates are likely significantly higher, while overhead may only be marginally more.

If we look at this method in the same scatter plot as before (Figure 3), we can again clearly see the issue with this approach. We have eliminated timekeepers with negative margins at standard but have replaced that with a large number of highly compensated timekeepers with margins exceeding 80 percent, while most of the lower-level timekeepers (presumably associates) have lower margins.

Hopefully the two examples above (while slightly extreme but based on real scenarios) have proven to you the need to have a more balanced approach to partner direct costs. To find this balance, the solution is to divide partner compensation into two buckets – one that is allocated as a direct cost to clients in the margin model, and the other that is captured "below the line". In some instances, I have seen firms ignore the latter bucket as their margin model had the singular purpose of evaluating clients and matters. In these instances, tying out to the general ledger was not necessary as the evaluation of attorney margins were viewed as too contentious to pursue. Once you have acknowledged that this is an issue that needs a solution, the questions becomes "How much is

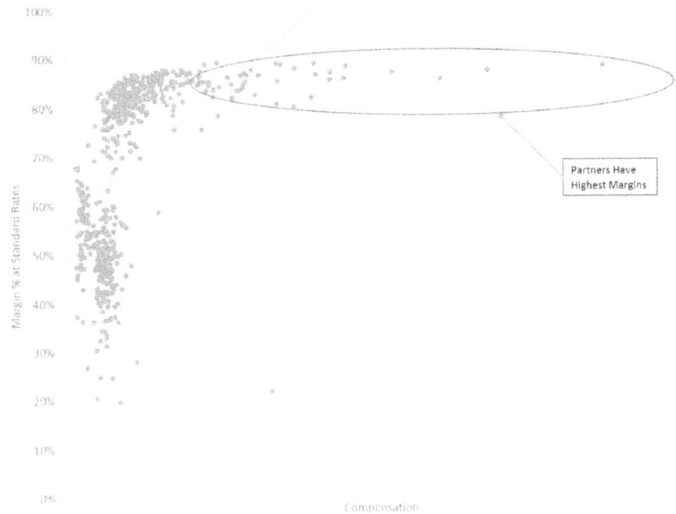

Figure 3: No partner direct costs

allocated to a client and how much is kept out?" and "How do I know if I have issues?"

Over the years, I have seen a number of methods for "capping" partner direct costs. Most have their merits and drawbacks but some are stronger than others. Below I will review these methods, their strengths and weaknesses, along with their risks associated with each. However, before we start discussing the specifics, we must have a set of criteria or guiding principles for our methodologies.

- Positive margins at standard rates. Total cost rate cannot exceed standard rate for timekeepers. Why would a firm set a standard rate such that it is losing money on each hour? Exceptions to the rule may exist for strategic investments in a practice, office, or industry group but they should be just that – an exception, not the rule. Even then, an argument can be made that this investment or loss-leader decision should be managed in alternative ways (discounts as an example). I would even take this a step further and suggest that the margins at standard rates need to be sufficient to handle reasonable discounting – should a five percent discount cause a negative margin?
- Incentivize a leverage model. For most timekeepers, margins (as a percentage of standard rates) decrease naturally as rates and compensation increase. This creates an incentive for utilizing less

experienced timekeepers where possible and ultimately increases the value to your clients. Does your methodology have continuity with other timekeepers and service partners?

- Keep it simple. Can it be effectively and efficiently managed on an ongoing basis? How will you support lateral partners and promotions? Can you easily explain it to a partner?
- Aligns with compensation system. Does your firm have an open or closed compensation system? Does this methodology make more information available than intended?
- Defensible and fair. Is your methodology artificially creating winners and losers within your firm? Can you defend the methodology to your partners?

Options

Direct cost cap

In this method, the firm creates a hard dollar cap for partners – any compensation above the cap is moved to the "below the line" bucket. For most firms, this cap has been a result of a compromise or what "feels" right. One firm with compensation determined by partner level essentially based the cap on a given level (partners above a level X get the same direct costs as all level X partners; partners below level X receive all compensation as a direct cost). Regardless of how the cap is derived, the result is the same. While at first this may seem like a reasonable approach, we will see a minor Midas effect for high rate partners along with a margin squeeze for partners with lower rates. In the example below (a $600,000 cap) we see Partner 2 with a zero percent standard margin while Partner 4 (a very experienced rainmaker in New York) has margins again approaching the associate in our first example.

	Partner 1	Partner 2	Partner 3	Partner 4
Rate	$475	$485	$550	$900
Compensation	$350,000	$600,000	$1,100,000	$2,000,000
Direct costs	$350,000	$600,000	$600,000	$600,000
Standard margin %	29%	0%	12%	46%

Looking at our scatter chart again (Figure 4), we can clearly see the two issues with this approach played out in the data. First, we still have some timekeepers with negative margins (although fewer than the fully loaded approach). Second, instead of seeing margins continue to decrease as compensation increases, we have the top half dozen partners with margins around the median for the entire firm (and above many associates).

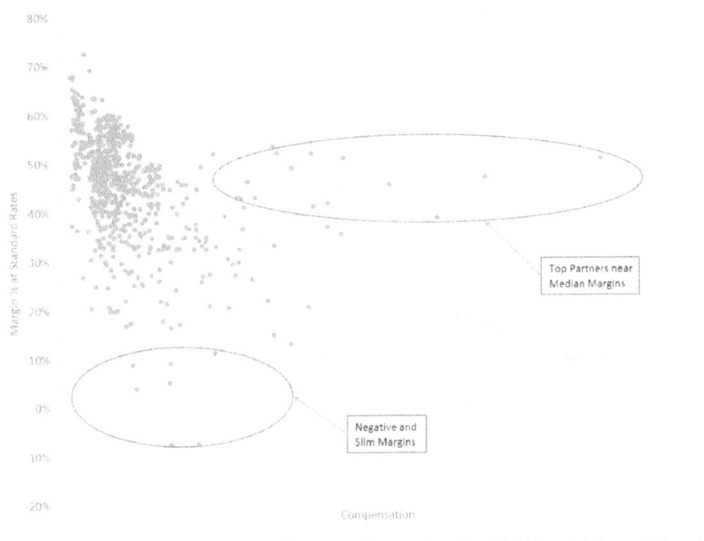

Figure 4: Direct cost cap

Minimum margin $

With this method, we simply define a minimum margin per hour as a dollar amount to guarantee a positive margin at standard rates. As an example, the firm may say that each hour should have at least $100 in margin at standard rates. If a partner's fully loaded costs produce a rate with more than $100 in margins, no adjustments are necessary. However, if the fully loaded cost rate is more than standard less $100, their cost rate will be capped. Looking at the same partner group from above shows no adjustment to Partner 1 but adjustments occurring for Partners 2, 3, and 4.

	Partner 1	Partner 2	Partner 3	Partner 4
Rate	$475	$485	$550	$900
Compensation	$350,000	$600,000	$1,100,000	$2,000,000
Fully loaded cost rate	$338	$485	$779	$1,309
Capped cost rate	$338	$385	$450	$800
Margin %	29%	21%	18%	11%

Also worth noting here is that, with this group, we are able to see diminishing margin percentages as both compensation and rates increase – exactly what we want to see if we are trying to encourage better leverage and value delivery to our clients (Partner 4 has the lowest margin and we would want to use him or her sparingly on matters).

With this methodology, we have accomplished the first two goals of a methodology – every timekeeper has positive margins and we clearly

Figure 5: Minimum margin $

see a downward trend in our scatter chart in Figure 5. Additionally, this method is not prohibitively complicated to implement or explain. So, depending on your firm, this might be a fundamentally solid option for addressing the issue at hand – more about that later.

Minimum margin %

This method is almost identical to the prior except instead of having a minimum margin defined in dollars, it is defined as a percentage. Here, the firm might decide that each timekeeper should have a margin of at least 15 percent at standard rates. Looking again at the four partners from our previous examples shows that we are again adjusting Partners 2, 3, and 4 and not adjusting Partner 1.

	Partner 1	Partner 2	Partner 3	Partner 4
Rate	$475	$485	$550	$900
Compensation	$350,000	$600,000	$1,100,000	$2,000,000
Fully loaded cost rate	$338	$485	$779	$1,309
Capped cost rate	$338	$412	$468	$765
Margin %	29%	15%	15%	15%

Through this table and the scatter diagram in Figure 6, we can see that while we don't have decreasing margins for the adjusted partners, the highest compensated and highest rate partners are held to a lower margin, thus maintaining an incentive for implementing a higher leverage model. As with the minimum margin $ method, we are again achieving the first two goals of this process, plus it is reasonably simple. Therefore, this again could be a valid and reasonable option for your firm.

With the previous two methods, we have achieved our primary objectives in a way that is defensible and fairly simple. So why is one of these not the recommended methodology? The simple answer is that the cost rates are based on standard rates. If your firm has consistent standard rates and realization across practices and offices, there may be no issue.

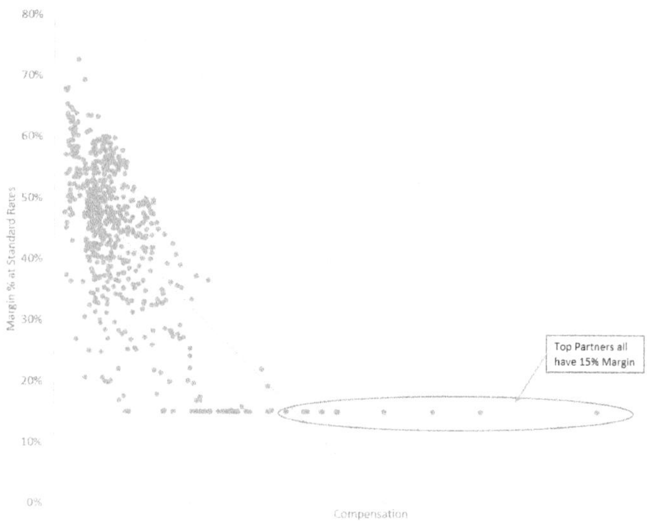

Figure 6: Minimum margin %

However, I have worked with and for firms that have recently undergone aggressive rate increases. When this happens, you inevitably have partners that agree to the increase but believe standard rates are "aspirational", while others are successful in avoiding the increase in an effort to salvage realization. If this dynamic exists at your firm, is it reasonable or fair for the more aggressive (some might call agreeable) partner to see their costs increase in tandem with their standard rates while their realized rates may only increase slightly?

To further illustrate this point, consider two partners below. Both have the same standard rate, effective rate, and compensation (that does need to be capped, in this example to have at least $150 in margin per hour). Going into the next fiscal year, Partner 1 agrees to an $800 standard rate ($100/14 percent increase) while Partner 2 only agrees to a $725 standard rate ($25/<4 percent increase). As a result of the more aggressive increase, Partner 1 sees a larger increase in effective rate (despite a slightly lower realization), which was the goal of the rate increase from the onset. However, because the methodology is based on standard rates, Partner 1's cost rate increased by $100 while Partner 2's cost rate only increased by $25. This results in lower margins for Partner 1 in year 2 despite the higher effective rate and the trust this partner put in finance with regards to their rate. This is obviously not the type of result we would want to create as it could create a disincentive to standard rate increases, despite research that shows the impact on effective billing rates and overall firm performance. If your firm is in a similar position, you will want to use or develop a methodology that is not based on the timekeepers' standard rates.

		Year 1	Year 2
Partner 1	STD rate	$700	$800
	Effective rate	$650	$700
	Cost rate	$550	$650
	Margin %	15%	7%
Partner 2	STD rate	$700	$725
	Effective rate	$650	$663
	Cost rate	$550	$575
	Margin %	15%	13%

Sliding scale

This approach is my favorite, despite the fact that it is more complex than the others (and that is its greatest weakness). This methodology was born of necessity after certain partners pushed back on the previous methods due to being rate-based. The theory for this approach is that the more a partner is compensated, the less of this compensation is likely due to their efforts as a working attorney. As such, direct costs can continue to increase with higher compensation levels but at a slower pace. There are many ways that a firm could implement such an approach. If your firm has partner levels with a set comp for each, it could be as simple as this:

Partner level	% of comp as direct cost
Level 1	100%
Level 2	100%
Level 3	100%
Level 4	90%
Level 5	80%
Level 6	70%
Level 7 and so on	

Without partner levels, a similar chart could be determined with comp ranges in place of the partner level. The only drawback could be "jumps" from one year to the next if a partner moves from one band higher or lower with only a slight change in compensation. If the threshold between 80 and 90 percent was $500k, a partner moving from $490k to $510k would actually see a decrease in direct costs from $441k (90 percent of $490k) to $408k (80 percent of $510k).

To avoid these "jumps", we took our cue from progressive income tax systems, where tax rates are only applied to income above the last threshold. Except in our case, the percentage of compensation recognized as a direct cost in our margin model is decreasing as income increases. This might look like the next table:

Comp mimimum	Comp maximum	Marginal % of comp as direct costs
	$A	100%
$A	$B	50%

$B	$C	30%
$C	$D	25%
	>$D	20%

Let's say that $A is $350k and a partner has compensation of $450k (which is less than the next threshold – $B). One hundred percent of the first $350k would be considered a direct cost but only 50 percent of the amount over $350k would be included. This gives us a total direct cost of $400k for this timekeeper – $350k plus 50 percent of $100k – with the remaining $50k going "below the line". Below are two charts illustrating how this would look in practice. In Figure 7, overleaf, we see that as compensation increases, the portion allocated as a cost decreases. Figure 8 shows the actual direct costs continuing to increase with compensation but at a slower pace. In both charts, we see that there are no jumps or sudden increases in direct costs that one might see as counter-intuitive.

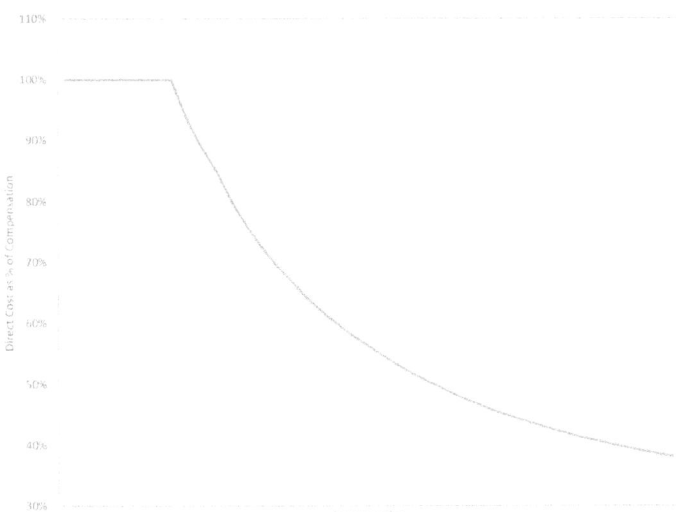

Figure 7: Direct cost as percentage of compensation

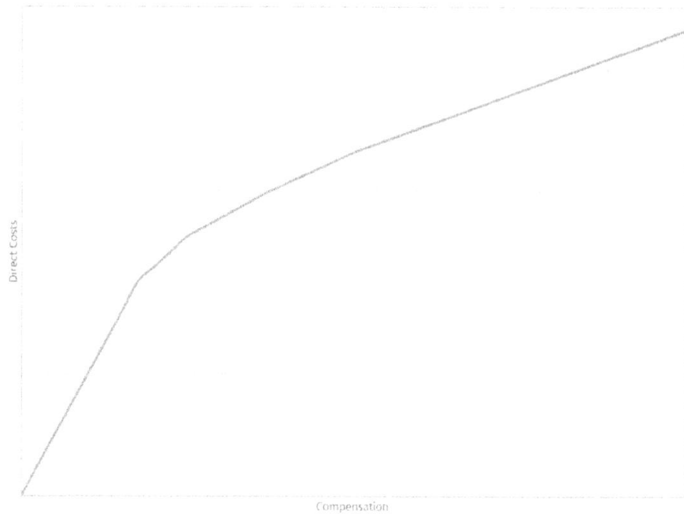

Figure 8: Actual direct costs

Looking now at our scatter chart for this methodology (Figure 9), we do have decreasing margins with increasing compensation and all time-keepers have positive margins. This has been accomplished without bringing rates into the conversation.

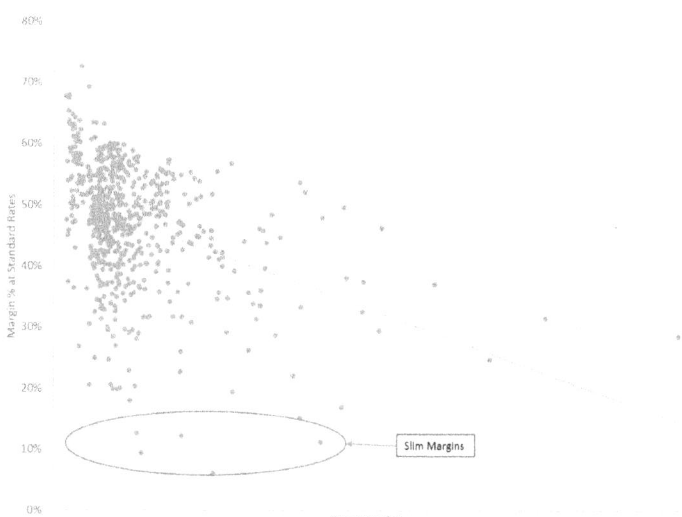

Figure 9: Sliding scale (marginal percentage)

We already know that the complexity could be an issue (though the partners I worked with greatly appreciated the innovativeness and novelty of this approach). However, aside from the complexity, there are two other issues. First, as in all of the other methods, the thresholds and marginal percentages could be seen as arbitrary, but instead of a single arbitrary number, we now have many. Second, while we have gotten all timekeepers to have positive margins, we still have two timekeepers below 10 percent and about a half dozen below 15 percent – is this acceptable? When I helped implement this in the past, we also utilized a 15 percent minimum to catch such outliers. However, this wasn't widely communicated to avoid confusion – we figured those partners wouldn't mind having a slightly more advantageous margin.

What next?

As I stated earlier, no perfect solution exists unless a firm explicitly breaks down compensation into each contributing factor and can come to consensus on which factors are and are not allocated to clients. In the absence of perfection, you must instead find out what works for your firm, its culture, and its landscape of partners (rates, compensation, etc.). Hopefully by seeing these approaches along with their strengths and flaws you are better equipped to develop such a solution for your firm or to be prepared for pushback and questions should they arise.

If you have not thought about the issue before or want to perform a sanity check on your firm, I suggest using the scatter chart we have used throughout this chapter and plot the margin at standard rates (1 – cost rate/standard rate) against compensation (standard rate could be effective as well). This will highlight the issues and timekeepers that may need attention. From there, don't be afraid to try the approaches above or to get creative – you might use one of the methods discussed, develop a hybrid of multiple approaches or come up with something new and better. Besides perhaps calculating the indirect costs per timekeeper (if you plan on using net margin), you do not need specialty software or tools to perform this analysis. Excel has more than enough power and flexibility for exploring multiple approaches on a single workbook.

Lastly, if you do not already have a small group of partners who understand the need for profitability and that you trust for feedback, start looking. Such a group of individuals is critical to getting other perspectives and, later, for building buy-in across the organization. Use them liberally – the right people will want to have input and will be more than willing to help.

Good luck and happy analyzing...

Chapter 7:
In favor of a client- and product-focused profitability analysis

By Thomas W Van Der Moere, chief financial officer at Neal, Gerber & Eisenberg LLP

Companies consistently face challenges and opportunities to enhance their business models and provide value to their customers, workforce, and owners. Law firms, of course, are no different. Firms need to address competition (for clients and talent) from traditional and non-traditional providers of legal services. They must grapple with the economic forces of supply and demand for legal products and services, as well as the complexity of responding to those forces through pricing and acquiring and maintaining the optimum mix and depth of talent. Firms face pressures to reshape their compensation structures to provide incentives that motivate a level of profitability that attracts, rewards, and retains key business generators and the workforce required to effectively support that business. In order to remain viable and competitive, a firm must decide where and how best to invest its limited available resources (i.e., its retained earnings/capital/debt) in technology, marketing, infrastructure, geographic presence, and talent. A firm that has a well-defined, flexible, and clearly understood profitability methodology, a culture that embraces a profitability mindset, and the ability to fully leverage that methodology when making decisions, will be better prepared to take advantage of the strategic challenges and opportunities it faces.

This chapter will focus on a law firm's opportunity to analyze existing and potential business using client and product profitability analysis. Too often, firms develop and deploy systems that are tilted toward a focus on analyzing the productivity of (billable hour) revenue contributed by timekeepers (individually or in the aggregate). Realigning that focus on the profitability of clients and the products the firm offers to its clients will lead to strategic insights into the factors/characteristics that are correlated with more profitable aspects of the firm's business. Understanding which revenue dollars drive firm profits and why will allow the firm to concentrate its efforts and direct its resources where the return on those resources can be maximized.

Client and product profitability – developing a methodology

As law firms build their understanding and sophistication in leveraging profitability analysis, its impact should be felt in several areas. Profitability analysis should affect talent acquisition and retention decisions. It should also influence the retention of clients and the acceptance of new clients. Compensation systems should be informed by contribution to the firm's profitability. The pricing of engagements and the overall pricing strategy of the firm require a deep understanding of the impact on profitability. Even the delivery of legal services to clients has to consider such factors of profitability as the efficiency and staffing mix of the service delivered, in addition to the quality of service delivered and the responsiveness of the law firm to its clients' needs.

A well-designed methodology that is deployed for a variety of purposes throughout the firm will also provide the added benefit of identifying opportunities to improve practices or address behavior issues that directly impact firm profitability.

Understanding how profitability will impact performance measurement and decision-making throughout the firm will guide the development and refinement of the firm's profitability methodology. The illustration below presents a typical profitability methodology that can be used at the firm, practice group, product, client or even individual timekeeper level. This conceptual diagram is also a way to illustrate

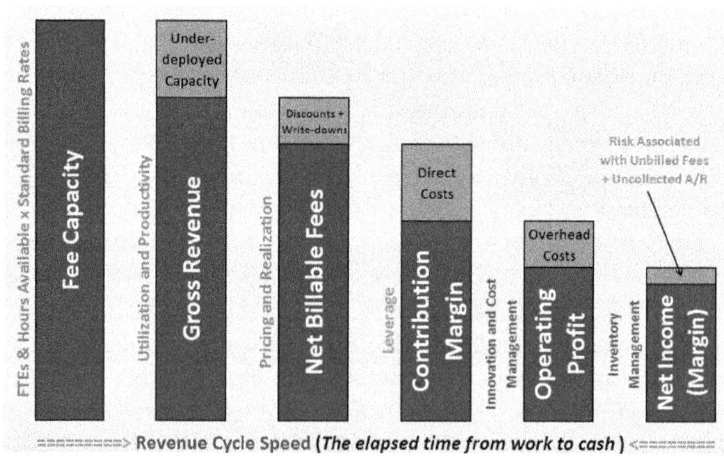

Figure 1: General segments of a profitability methodology

– not only to attorneys, but also to administrative department leadership and finance staff – how each member of staff can directly or indirectly impact the profitability of the firm.

This methodology begins with some concept of the fee-generating capacity applicable to what is being measured. This can be defined a number of ways, depending on the operations of the firm, but the conceptually simple calculation is to determine the hours capacity available multiplied by the average standard billing rate offered to clients (full-time equivalent timekeepers x the standard billable hours expectations for the timekeepers x the timekeepers' standard billing rate).

All firms experience a leakage of that fee capacity from a variety of sources. Timekeepers that are undisciplined recorders of time fail to capture all of the effort they spend on a client's matter or even self-discount their time (from the unease at appearing as inefficient) by not recording time for which they perceive the client will not pay or will challenge.

Leakage of fee capacity can also be derived from how resources are managed and deployed throughout the firm. Larger practice areas within a firm may suffer from being a loosely-connected group of sole practitioners, even if those practitioners are essentially delivering the same product to clients. If each practitioner requires their own team to service clients, and there is no disciplined resource management practice in place to ensure that available resources are fully utilized across the practice, it is likely that almost all timekeepers are contributing some level of fee capacity leakage that, when added up across the practice, is significant lost profit potential. Don't get me wrong – 100 percent or greater utilization of a firm's resources is highly unlikely and probably not desirable over the long run. Having an appropriate level of bench strength in certain practices is also required in situations where client demand can be volatile or is needed to maintain a perceived ability to handle larger client matters. However, a more disciplined approach to managing the allocation of work among available resources to ensure they are sufficiently utilized will have a material impact on the firm's profit.

The next factor in the profitability continuum is the fee discounts agreed with clients and the writing-down of fees prior to preparing the invoice to the client. The result is the net billable fees that the firm passes on to clients.

As noted at the bottom of Figure 1, profitability is impacted by the work-to-cash cycle time. Often referred to as bill-speed and collection-speed, this is the amount of time that elapses from when the work was performed to when the firm receives payment for its services from clients. The speed at which recorded time is converted to billed fees and the billed fees are converted to cash received by the firm can have direct profitability implications as well as indirect consequences. Because of the need to carry this investment related to unconverted work-to-cash, if a firm needs to draw upon its line of credit to fund continuing operations, the borrowing costs will be a direct overhead expense. The speed of this conversion could also create a requirement for partner capital investment or could result in delayed distributions of profit to the partners.

Costs come from direct sources associated with the firm's revenue producers (partner salaries, non-partner attorney and paralegal compensation, benefits and payroll taxes paid by the firm) and indirect sources or overhead (i.e., the costs to operate the firm such as occupancy costs, administrative department costs, professional liability insurance, etc.). A good profitability model can assist in highlighting where leverage, staffing mix, and compensation adjustments could improve profit margins by better aligning costs with the firm's revenue potential. A profitability model can not only inform revenue producers of the firm as to where opportunities exist to improve client and product profitability, but it can also be used by administrative department management to better understand how the processes and costs that they manage have a significant impact on the firm's profitability. Tying the impact of process improvement initiatives, innovation, technology enhancements, and cost management programs back to the profitability of client engagements, practices, and the firm is powerful support for the projects, initiatives, and resources requested by the firm's administrative support departments.

Lastly, leakage of potential revenue comes from the write-off of uncollected accounts receivable and time and costs that age as work-in-process and are eventually written off. Good inventory management practices that include frequent monitoring, measurement, and notification of potential issues, as well as a collaborative and coordinated effort between your firm's finance staff and billing attorneys, is essential to limiting the impact of this material profit leak.

The table below provides a simple illustration of the basic methodology that could apply to results at the firm, practice, office, client/matter, product, or timekeeper level.

Timekeeper FTEs	300	85	Equity partners
Hours available	525,000		
Fee capacity (at standard rates)	$263,000,000	$500	Weighted average of all timekeepers' standard rates
Unused capacity	80,000	15%	
	($40,000,000)		
Gross revenue (at standard rates)	$223,000,000	445,000	Client billable hours
Discounts and write-downs	($33,000,000)	(15%)	
Net billable fees	$190,000,000		
Direct costs	($90,000,000)	(40%)	Assumes average base direct cost per equity partner of $350,000
Contribution margin	$100,000,000		
Overhead costs	($70,000,000)	(31%)	
Operating profit	$30,000,000		
Client invest-ment costs	$4,500,000	(2%)	Time that remains unbilled, uncollected A/R, cost/disburse-ment write-offs etc
Net income (margin)	$25,500,000	11%	

Figure 2: A basic profitability calculation

Client and product profitability analysis

In most law firms today, you will hear varying levels of claims that they are client-focused and provide their clients with quality service. This should be a priority for law firms. Competition for client business is fierce. Non-traditional service providers are entering the market, as they see opportunities to take market share from traditional law firms and do so profitably. Clients are much more sophisticated and aggressive in their procurement of legal services and demand more value from their providers. Clients want different prices for different products provided by their law firms based on the value they receive from those products.

Despite this shift in focus to the client and the products they consume, many law firm financial and practice management systems are rooted primarily in the firm, practice groups and departments, offices and regions, and attorneys/timekeepers rather than clients and the firm's products. Some of this is driven by traditional accounting-based roll-ups of cost and revenue centers as well as partner compensation and other incentive systems. Any client-focused analysis tends to stop at revenue and revenue in process (accounts receivable and unbilled time). Product analysis, if done, is likely to only have a revenue-based focus, and is most likely in response to developing an alternative fee arrangement requested by a client.

The constant struggle to grow demand and revenue, in part to absorb the timekeeper capacity that many firms have maintained as well as the pricing pressures exerted by clients, has clouded the focus on profitability somewhat. Intuitively, law firm leaders realize that not all dollars of revenue contribute an equal amount of profit to the firm. However, firms' profitability models and analyses need to shift the focus to understanding that statement in the context of their clients and the firm's products. A system that facilitates this analysis across the firm's existing client base, its various types of matters/services from its practices, and acceptance of new client business will position the firm to better address the profit leakages discussed above, better inform pricing and fee arrangements, create a clearer understanding of the underlying cost drivers in the delivery of legal services, and inform decisions as to which and what types of clients and mix of firm services require the firm's resources and continued investment.

These client- and product-focused profitability models must highlight:

- Differences in the prices charged to different clients;
- Discounts or other forms of revenue support required by clients;

- Differences in the products/services delivered to different clients;
- Differences in the amount of resources consumed across clients;
- Whether the firm is working with decision-makers at the client or if decisions need to be made up the chain of command;
- The level of support required by clients (do some require large teams? Are some clients less sophisticated or require more touch points? What is the breadth and focus of the client's internal legal team?); and
- The industries in which firm clients operate (are there common characteristics/factors that drive client or product profitability by industry?).

The direct benefits of client- and product-profitability analysis lie in the insight it provides in the uneven distribution of revenue and costs among clients and the firm's products. The insight gained from this analysis regarding the extent to which specific customers, types of customers, and products consume the firm's resources should generate opportunities for the firm in better management of costs, better informed pricing and revenue generation, and concentrated strategic marketing activities.

Considerations for developing a profitability methodology for clients and products

I do not plan to address basic design elements of a profitability model and system, as that is addressed substantially in a number of texts and articles (for example, the best method to use to allocate overhead costs). However, there are several key elements that deserve mention as they will help develop a model that facilitates client and product profitability analysis. Overall, you need to design a model and system that is flexible, and can be customized and adjusted to fit how you want to use it within your firm. Make sure you have thought through your data sources (general ledger, payroll system, other external sources of cost, revenues, full-time equivalents, etc.) and have developed a mapping to your profitability system that contains the level of granularity (or summarization) that fits your particular firm's needs. For example, if your model includes an extensive breakdown of overhead costs, you may invite greater debate from your attorneys on whether they are a consumer of that cost to the same extent as another attorney.

Some of the areas that have particular relevance to client and product profitability analysis are the measurement period basis, how you factor in partner compensation, the need for reconciling the profit data to your general ledger, product designations, and cost rates.

Measurement period basis

An important distinction to make in the profitability model for analyzing client and product profitability is the basis to use for the measurement period. The accounting rule of matching revenues with costs applies here as well. The two basic periods to consider are the "worked period" and the "collected period". The worked period basis focuses on the costs that are associated with the work done (recorded) during the measurement period. The collected period basis focuses on the revenue (fees collected) during the measurement period.

Since the worked period basis starts with the actual time recorded and costs incurred, you must identify the revenues directly associated with that time/cost. Depending on when you are analyzing the worked period data, the associated revenues are likely in different stages of being converted to cash:

- A portion of the time/fees has been billed and collected (revenue);
- A portion of the time/fees has been billed, but remains uncollected (accounts receivable); and
- A portion of the time/fees remains unbilled (work-in-process).

Given the last two stages represent a transition to cash, you must develop assumptions that reflect some degree of risk that the amounts do not convert to cash/revenue. Although you could choose to develop your model to exclude inventory (A/R and WIP) from revenue, it probably does not make sense to do so for client and product profitability analysis (it may, if you feel it is appropriate for individual timekeeper or practice group profitability – creating an incentive to collect). For client and product profitability, determining some methodology for setting collection risk and billing risk to apply to time/fees that are in the A/R and WIP stages, respectively, is most effective. A basic methodology involves an analysis of historical realizations and/or the likely conversion to cash based on the historical aging of the firm's/client's A/R and WIP.

The collected period basis starts with revenue (fees collected) produced in the measurement period. If you use the costs from the measurement period, you will not achieve a matching of costs and revenue (i.e. different costs were incurred to produce the revenue you are collecting in the measurement period) – not ideal for meaningful client and product profitability analysis. You must, therefore, try to develop a methodology that identifies costs associated to the period from which the revenue originated. When write-downs occurred or A/R and WIP still exist related to that revenue, you must be certain your methodology is not over- or under-allocating costs to the measurement period and misstating profitability.

For the purposes of client and product profitability, the worked period basis would tend to be the preferable method, because of the importance of understanding the true amount of effort and cost absorbed in servicing the client and delivering the product during the measurement period.

Partner compensation

Should partner compensation (draws/distributions/bonuses) be considered a cost or is it just profit? For client and product profitability (and maybe for most law firm profitability models), I think it makes sense to include some portion of what a partner receives as a direct cost to the profitability model. Most firms should be able to agree upon a reasonable amount to associate to a partner as a direct salary cost. This direct salary cost does not have to be, and in most cases should not be, the partners' draw amount. The amount of the partners' total compensation and the direct salary cost can be captured separately and included if important to the type of profitability analysis that is being performed. For client and product profitability, any compensation above the direct salary cost should be excluded. Including the profit that was produced during the measurement period as a cost to the client or product being analyzed distorts the results.

Reconciliation of the profitability model to the general ledger

In the abstract, reconciling your profitability data to the income statement generated from your general ledger sounds like a prudent exercise to ensure the data's accuracy. Your controller will likely roll his or her eyes at the suggestion that you would not do so. However, you should seriously consider not forcing a reconciliation to the general ledger. Of course, it will depend on the types of profitability analyses you will be performing and whether or not your organization requires that the two sets of data tie out perfectly.

Here are some benefits and issues related to each:

	Benefit	Issue
Reconciliation	Reconciliation to the income statement may help obtain buy-in from skeptical partners about the accuracy of the profitability data you are relating to them, their clients, their practice, etc.	There may be costs that you do not want to include in profitability analyses. For example, one-time charges or other costs incurred that are not part of normal operations. There are likely to be frequent situations where you may want to spread the impact of certain costs over multiple periods for profitability analysis. For example, if you wish to include in your profitability model any bonuses paid to associates or staff, which are paid (and hit the GL) in December, you may want to spread these amounts over an entire calendar year period. Some firms may want to reflect certain revenues as an offset to expenses (i.e., any revenue produced by the billing of library research staff related to a client engagement is offset against the cost of that administrative area).
No reconciliation	Flexibility through fewer restrictions on how you use various components of revenue and cost to inform the profitability model and leverage it for multiple purposes.	Being prepared to easily explain how not tying out exactly to the firm's financial statement net income is OK and is unnecessary to effectively use the results of the profitability models.

Product designations

Law firms have products to sell. Those products are developed through varied processes (using different resources and costs), are often priced differently, are marketed differently, and present widely varying client demand scenarios for firms. Consequently, they contribute to a law firm's revenue and profitability uniquely as well. We should, therefore, measure the profit contribution of those products to better assess which products carry the highest margin potential and where opportunities for cost efficiencies, tailored pricing, and demand creation exist.

It is strongly encouraged that you develop a set of product codes (or areas of practice or however the firm wishes to label them) that you attach as part of the metadata you assign to matter records. These should be matter designations that represent unique categories of matters on which you typically work for your clients. If you make the designation too broad, it will become difficult to wade through the volume of data (i.e., time records) to isolate the drivers of effort/cost for the matter. You may also lose the ability to better identify opportunities to price the stages or phases of a matter differently, which may give you an edge in securing work from a client or in demonstrating value more clearly. For example, if your only product designation for corporate and securities matters was a single "corporate" designation, you are potentially restricting your ability to fully understand the underlying cost drivers of this collection of engagements with clients. By grouping your matters into slightly more specific segments – such as M&A, public company securities, venture capital, etc. – you have an opportunity (perhaps coupled with some well-defined and easy to implement matter phase/task codes) to cost and price work that aligns with what your client sees as your product offering to them. The extension is to then analyze the relative profit contribution of various product segments or of the profit contribution of a single product across the client base. A practice that has the ability to analyze the pattern of effort and cost to deliver its products, will more readily be able to identify opportunities to increase efficiency and reduce costs, and, in turn, have the confidence and flexibility to offer fee arrangements to better meet their clients' value expectations.

Cost rates (standard vs full)

As client and product profitability analysis is reliant on the underlying cost data and assumptions, establishing a basis for cost rates is important to the methodology. Cost rate data not only informs the analysis of historical results, but is important in developing predictive models of profitability and "what-if" planning scenarios. So, should cost rates be based on a pre-defined number of standard hours per timekeeper? In other words, should we create a standard-cost rate that ignores whether one timekeeper is "busier" or more fully deployed than another? Alternatively, should cost rates be based on the actual hours worked by a timekeeper? Some firms refer to this as a full-cost rate because it includes the cost of carrying excess capacity (the difference between a standard hours target and actual hours recorded).

Although the full-cost rate has its purpose, it should not necessarily be used for client and product profitability analysis. The full-cost rate is useful in situations where you are analyzing the profitability of an organizational unit (i.e., the working results of a practice group or the firm as a whole) or an individual working timekeeper.

For most client and product profitability analyses, the standard-cost rate approach provides for stronger comparability across clients and products. In other words, two attorneys with identical salaries and benefits and billing rates would produce the same amount of profit per hour recorded, regardless of whether one was 100 percent utilized and the other was 80 percent utilized. The standard-cost rate approach does not penalize or burden a client or product with the cost associated with carrying excess capacity within a practice or across the firm.

Having spent some time discussing conceptually the uses of client and product profitability analysis as well as considerations in developing a methodology, let's take a look at a simple case study that provides a basis for leveraging client and product profitability analysis to support business decision-making.

Case study

The following case study provides some insight into the mechanics of implementing client and product profitability analysis. The firm in the case study – Van Treist, McCallen & Holland – is a fictitious 300-timekeeper firm principally based in Minneapolis, but with several offices in the Midwest and an office in the Miami area. The firm has transactional- and controversy-based practices and a broad and diversified client base. The clients represent many industries and are a mix of public and privately held companies and individuals.

The last eight weeks had been some of the most unpleasant of Susan Driver's career. The annual compensation process for the partners of the firm had just wrapped up and final bonus compensation had been disclosed to partners almost a week prior. The discussions during (and outside of) the compensation committee meetings had, in many cases, been particularly contentious and personal. The bonus pool was smaller this past year, and had been gradually declining for the past four to five years. Some areas of the firm were doing fairly well, maintaining or increasing revenue slightly. However, other areas were experiencing slight to moderate pressure on demand for services and lower overall revenues per client. As with many firms their size, the firm was also struggling to manage increasing costs, the need to invest in technology and business development, and manage overcapacity across the firm. These factors were all contributing to an uneasiness throughout the partner ranks and was clearly behind the difficulties experienced during this year's compensation discussions.

Sitting in her office in the evening of another long day, the firm's managing partner reread a couple of emails she had received earlier in the day from two of the firm's prominent partners. The first email was from Mark Janseits, the co-leader of the litigation practice:

"Many of the partners in this practice that I have talked to over the last several days are very displeased with their final compensation for the year, and raised concerns over the lack of growth of our firm in both demand for our services and the income available to the partnership. Although I do not think that any of them are immediate 'flight risks', I think we need to take steps to better understand what we need to do to improve our results as a firm and retain our top talent. Our focus should be on revenue generation. Perhaps it is time to more significantly raise our billing rates, even if it means our realizations will drop a bit further than they have already. I think we also just need to tell people to get off their chairs and go get more business. We also seem a bit heavy on administrative staff – a little more cost-cutting can't hurt. Let me know what I can do to help."

The second email had come from Laura Dennison. Laura and Susan had joined the same large multi-national law firm as associates over 20 years ago. They both left that firm around the same time. Laura went in-house at a former client, while Susan went to another large law firm, eventually landed at Van Treist, McCallen & Holland (VMH) about 12 years ago and became managing partner in 2016. Laura was recruited by Susan last year to lead the firm's private equity practice. Susan had always respected Laura's opinion and often sought her perspective on various issues she encountered in both her practice and in managing the firm. Laura wrote:

"I know you are probably bearing the brunt of the grumbling about the results of this year's partner compensation – I know I'm hearing my fair share! Don't get discouraged. Look, I think under your leadership, we have truly started to turn the focus of the firm towards the keys for improving our competitive position in the marketplace – emphasizing productivity and innovation, bringing structure and focus to our business development efforts, investing in technology and talent to meet our clients' needs, improving client communication, etc. These take time to bear fruit of course… and we at VMH are not the most patient folks in the world.

"And at least the concept of profitability has entered our lexicon and we've started to calculate it in terms of individual partner and practice group performance. However, I think we need to take it to the next level. We need to realize that not every dollar of revenue we collect from our clients contributes equally to the firm's profits. I'll be the first to admit that I have taken on some clients that consume a lot of my and my team's time, but for a small amount of fees or at a steep discount. But when we are measured heavily on the hours and revenue we generate, our perspectives (and decisions) get distorted. What I'm trying to say is that maybe our focus should shift from our practice groups, offices, and individual partners to our clients and the products/services we offer them. Which clients and services contribute (or could potentially contribute) higher profit margins to the firm and why? If we can then leverage that analysis to divert our resources to attracting and retaining like clients or deliver our services more profitably, how can our results not improve? I'd love to hear what your thoughts are on this."

Throughout the day, Susan had been jotting down her thoughts about what the firm should do and came to a similar conclusion – a greater focus on the firm's clients and the firm's products and how they contribute to overall profitability was probably a good place to start. As Mark suggested, rate adjustments, building better business development capabilities throughout the firm, and cost management certainly should to some extent be addressed. However, Susan was persuaded by Laura's idea to look at the profitability of the firm's clients and products. Would it not potentially yield the information necessary to identify opportunities for the firm to improve results, as well as informing more targeted adjustments to pricing, where to focus the firm's business development efforts, and better utilize resources and costs? She formulated those thoughts into four goals for the firm, leveraging profitability analysis:

- An improved understanding of the firm's sources of profitability;
- An improved understanding of the relationship between the characteristics of clients, products and costs;
- An improved understanding of the relationship between behaviors of timekeepers, staff and costs; and
- Better informed decisions about the allocation of resources to clients, types of clients, and products.

As Susan packed up for the evening commute home, she considered her next steps. On the ride home she wondered whether the firm had the systems, capabilities, and data to undertake this type of analysis. Later that night she sent a meeting notice to her heads of operations and finance to better understand what it would take to accomplish her objectives.

Response to case study

Susan and VMH are struggling with what most other law firms, to varying degrees, are facing. Simply raising rates is no longer a sustainable long-term strategy to increase profit. Firms have or are addressing fixed and variable overhead costs. Getting their arms around how and what clients and the products they purchase contribute value to the firm is an essential undertaking for any firm looking to compete in today's legal industry. To start this process at VMH, Susan and her team should follow this basic framework for their client and product profitability initiative:

- Selection of existing clients and products;
- Design the profitability model;
- Calculate the client and product profitability;
- Interpret the profitability results; and
- Establish the ability to perform client and product profitability analysis on a consistent, repeatable and regular basis.

Susan's goals for the firm's profitability analysis study are appropriately focused on obtaining the information she and the firm's leaders need to begin to understand which clients and products consume the firm's resources and where those resources have an uneven relationship to the revenues they generate. Identifying the targets for cost management and profit improvement initiatives that will contribute the most significant opportunities to impact the firm's profitability is the direct benefit of a client- and product-driven profitability analysis. Those clients that are highly profitable must be retained. Small, unprofitable customers that have limited potential to improve or grow (i.e., lead to more profitable work) should be referred to firms more suited to service the client. Small or less profitable clients (with potential to grow into more profitable clients) may require development programs to improve their profit contribution to the firm. This analysis can be similarly applied to the firm's products, and can be especially informative if it can be accomplished in combination with the clients that procure them.

Susan should consider forming a team that includes marketing, finance, knowledge management and, if appropriate and manageable, select attorneys. From there, the first step will be a thorough review of the firm's current active clients. A good place to start may be to try to segment clients based on some measure of volume/size and profitability. The table in Figure 3 is an example of a simple segmentation of the VMH firm data based on client size.

	Large	Mid-sized	Small	Total
Number of clients	100	250	1,500	1,850
Billable hours generated	180,000	160,000	90,000	430,000
Fees at standard rates	$125,000,000	£100,000,000	$55,000,000	$280,000,000
Fees generated	$110,000,000	$82,000,000	$44,000,000	$246,000,000
Average standard rate	$690	$630	$610	$650
Average effective rate	$610	$510	$490	$550
Realization vs standard rate	88%	82%	80%	84%
Fees per client	$1,100,000	$328,000	$29,333	$127.568
Direct costs	$55,000,000	$48,000,000	$27,500,000	$130,500,000
Allocated overhead costs	$24,750,000	$21,600,000	$12,500,000	$58,850,000
Total costs	$79,750,000	$69,600,000	$40,000,000	$189,350,000
Profit	$30,250,000	$12,400,000	$4,000,000	$46,650,000
Profit margin % (vs standard)	24%	12%	7%	17%

Percentage	Large	Mid-sized	Small
Number of clients	5%	14%	81%
Billable hours generated	42%	37%	21%
Fees at standard rates	45%	36%	20%
Fees generated	47%	35%	195
Profit	65%	27%	9%

Figure 3: High-level segmentation of the client base

This simple analysis provides some perspective on the firm's client base in terms of clients' consumption of firm resources and the corresponding profitability contribution of clients. As shown in the bottom table of this chart, the firm's clients form a pyramid whose base is made up of 80 percent of its clients who consume more than 20 percent of the firm's effort, but contribute less than 10 percent of the firm's profits. The top of the pyramid contains five percent of the firm's clients, but they contribute 65 percent of the firm's profit.

Design of the profitability model

The level of detail captured by and the design of VMH's profitability analysis system should be sufficient to at least produce the type of high-level analysis shown in the previous table, and to produce information on revenue and costs associated with each client.

If the firm has data such as industry classification or the area of practice (product designations) tagged to its matter records, this data can be further segmented by those attributes. VMH's profitability analysis will be much more useful to its decision-makers if the analysis can draw correlations to its profit contribution and certain client characteristics, such as:

- The client's industry;
- The level of the client's decision-makers with whom the firm has the strongest relationship (i.e. is the responsible partner's relationship with the client's general counsel, CEO, or owner, or is it with a mid-level manager or someone on the GC's team?);
- Length of client relationship with the firm;
- Client financial risk/stability; and
- Types and breadth of products purchased from the firm.

If VMH does not have a sufficient breakdown of its products, client industry, and other attributes that the firm believes would inform its analyses, and/or this data is not reflected in its profitability analysis system, Susan should at least consider (in the short term) associating these designations with a selected subset of the clients she wishes to analyze. This will be a bit of a manual effort, but can be accomplished over a smaller sample of clients. To build out its longer-term profitability analysis capabilities, the firm should then consider backfilling this data in its practice management or other central client/matter system for a larger set of clients as well as capturing this information through its new business intake process.

If the firm's data is not sufficiently broken down into products (areas of practice) at the matter level or by some level of phase or task for a matter, meeting the objective of the client and product profitability analysis to understand what drives the underlying costs will be difficult. Where this detail is not available – and even in cases where it is – the firm will need to resort to an analysis of time records. Of course, the better the quality of the narratives of those time records, the easier it will be to categorize them into the cost drivers that will inform this analysis. If a review of time records is required, I would suggest making the investment in one of several business intelligence software applications on the market that apply natural language processing algorithms to read timecard narratives. These applications can not only enhance your profitability analysis capabilities, but can provide better data more quickly for planning and pricing matters and projects for clients.

Profitability analysis

Below is a simple illustration of how VMH might start its client profitability analysis once it has segmented its clients by size or revenue contribution. This illustration focuses on the top 20 clients for VMH in its "large" client segment. Five metrics associated with the most recent annual period are extracted (If more meaningful, the data could be extracted for multiple periods and aggregated – whatever provides the best representation of the clients' consumption of firm resources and the associated revenue and profitability for the client). The metrics provided are:

- Potential fees – hours recorded valued at standard bill rates;
- Expected fee revenue – reflects the impact of client discounts, write-downs, and potential for not collecting accounts receivable or unbilled time;
- Expected realization percentage – the ratio of expected fee revenue to fees at standard rates;
- Profit margin – the expected fee revenue less the direct and indirect costs consumed by the client; and
- Profit margin percentage – the ratio of the profit margin to fees at standard rates.

Client	Fees at standard rates	Expected fee revenue	Realization %	Profit margin	Profit margin %
A	$4,250,000	$3,750,000	88%	$950,000	22%
B	$3,450,000	$2,850,000	83%	$700,000	20%
C	$2,500,000	$2,000,000	80%	$475,000	19%
D	$2,300,000	$2,150,000	93%	$675,000	29%
E	$2,200,000	$2,100,000	95%	$725,000	33%
F	$1,900,000	$1,850,000	97%	$675,000	36%
G	$1,850,000	$1,700,000	92%	$325,000	18%
H	$1,750,000	$1,550,000	89%	$500,000	29%

I	$1,750,000	$1,500,000	86%	$425,000	24%
J	$1,450,000	$1,250,000	86%	$200,000	14%
K	$1,400,000	$1,100,000	79%	$125,000	9%
L	$1,325,000	$1,250,000	94%	$375,000	28%
M	$1,200,000	$1,050,000	88%	$300,000	25%
N	$1,125,000	$950,000	84%	$225,000	20%
O	$1,000,000	$990,000	99%	$400,000	40%
P	$975,000	$800,000	82%	£250,000	26%
Q	$960,000	$875,000	91%	$175,000	18%
R	$800,000	$725,000	91%	$100,000	13%
S	$800,000	$650,000	81%	$175,000	22%
T	$725,000	$700,000	97%	$75,000	10%

Figure 4: Top 20 client profitability metrics

Figure 5 compares the clients, ordered by potential fees, and with comparisons to expected fee revenue and profit margin.

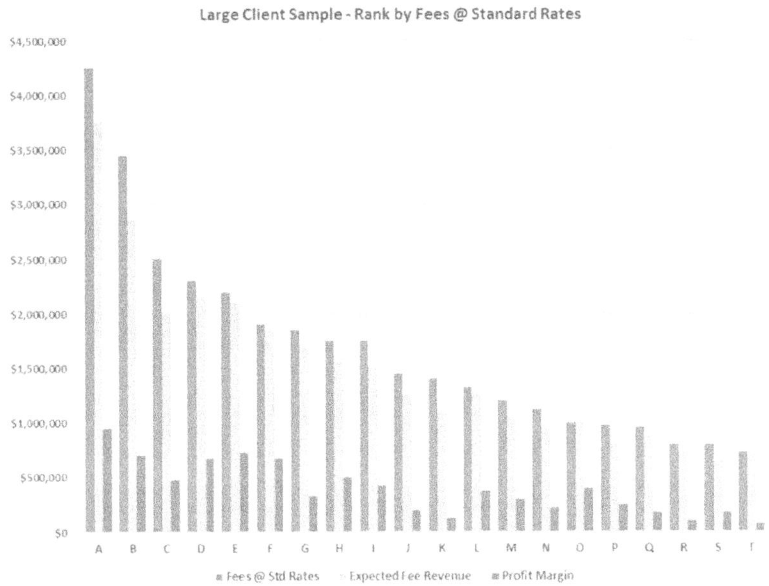

Figure 5: Client ranking by fees at standard rates.

Figure 6 presents the clients by the amount of profit margin each contributes.

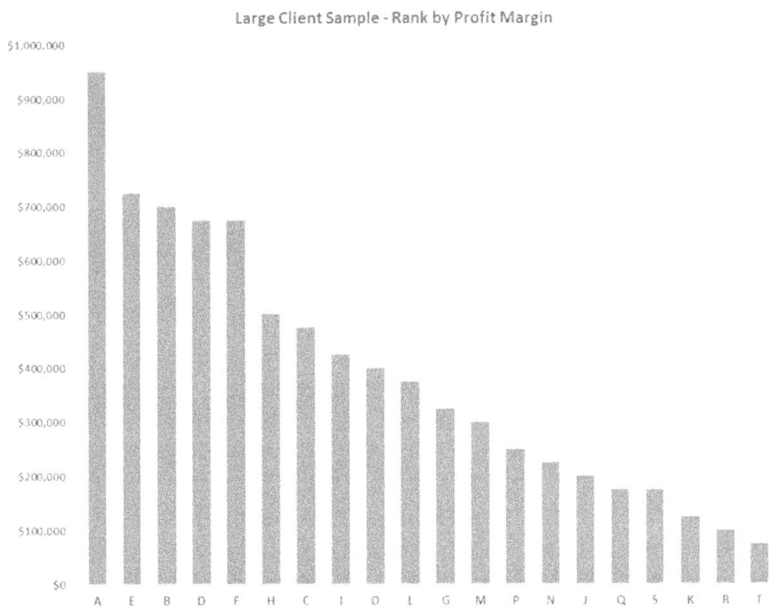

Figure 6: Client ranking by profit margin.

Figure 7 ranks the 20 clients based on profit margin percentage.

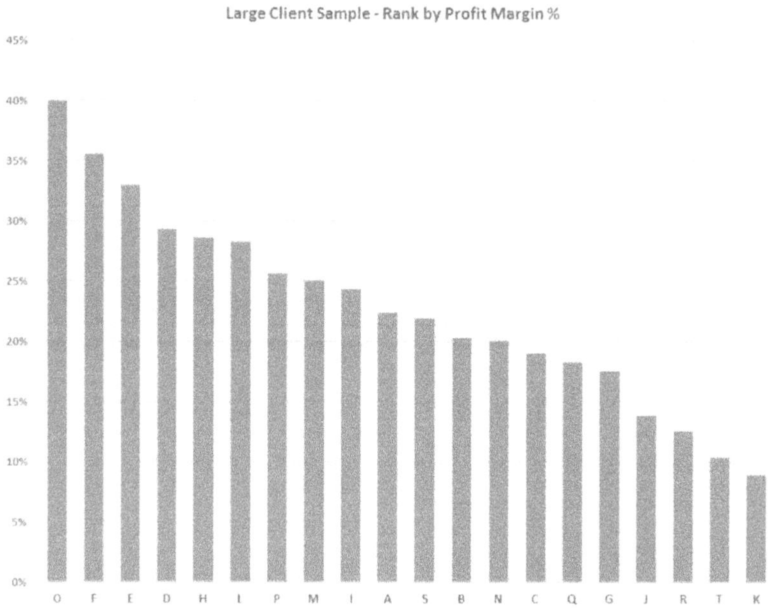

Figure 7: Client ranking by profit margin percentage.

These simple charts provide some interesting information regarding some of the basic drivers of profitability within this segment of VMH's clients. You can begin to see which clients are carrying larger client discounts or are experiencing write-downs and other value adjustments, or which clients seem to absorb more resources and hence costs. These are all, of course, key clients for the firm, but also offer the greatest opportunity to make meaningful profitability improvements, adjust client retention and service strategies, or inform other profitability improvement opportunities across the firm's client portfolio.

Conclusion

This study of VMH provides a general framework and approach for undertaking a deep analysis of a firm's clients and products and segmenting those clients/products based on profitability and value to the firm. Identifying opportunities for redirecting resources to more profitable activities, and implementing cost management and revenue enhancement initiatives, is the intent of this analysis. Although the client and product profitability analysis process will provide VMH with a useful assessment of which clients and products are most profitable and which are not, the firm should carefully use this information when considering the value of the relationship with any client. Profitability alone may not be the only factor that gives a client value to the firm. An unprofitable client could provide sufficient value if it has the opportunity to provide future profitability growth, could lead to access or referral to other more profitable clients, strengthens the firm's presence in a certain market segment, is associated in a meaningful way with another key firm client or influencer, etc. Again, the observation that not all revenue contributes equally to profitability (or more broadly, value) has meaning in this sense.

VMH will be using their profitability analyses to identify where consumption of firm resources, and therefore cost, is misaligned with the revenues generated. Those observations may lead the firm to consider pursuing changes to its strategy, investments, procedures, and processes in order to improve profitability. It needs to be mindful that its cost structure will determine how overall results will be impacted by those changes. For example, if it is determined that less profitable or smaller clients will be transitioned to another firm, the costs historically associated with those clients will still exist. Unless those resources are redeployed to other revenue-producing (and profit-accretive) assignments, no cost has left VMH's operations. Likewise, VMH will need to consider how changes in strategy, procedure, and process will impact fixed overhead costs.

A well-designed and implemented client and product profitability model and the analysis it facilitates will provide the firm with valuable information on which it can take action. Further value can come from an extension of this historical-based analytical process to one that is prospective. The data developed from the historical-based process should provide the firm with the intelligence to project and model future revenue, cost and profit profiles for existing and potential clients, client segments and products.

Chapter 8: Strategic approaches to improve firm financials

By Eddie Raychaudhuri, chief pricing and LPM officer

By this stage in your profitability rollout, you've put in the hard work and have gained the respect and support of your firm's management team. Assuming that there is an agreed-upon profitability methodology in place, what should you do with the numbers?

Initially (which can range from six months to two years), encourage management to mention matter profitability at all their meetings, from meetings with others in management to meetings where partners will be present. This will, over the long run, help create a culture where the word "profit" is not shied away from, and instead becomes second nature. When the support of management has been achieved and a profit methodology established, what is to be done with the results?

Matter approval process

During the client intake process, all new matters that are above a certain anticipated dollar threshold, or under any type of alternative fee arrangement, should be required to have a budget put together by the pricing team in conjunction with the billing partner. This budget should include projected profit results. During the course, and at the end, of the matter, actual profitability should be compared versus the budget, with accompanying variance reports with explanations. This will increase traction and visibility for the pricing/LPM group.

Set goal metrics

Lawyers are competitive by nature, so take advantage of this by setting goal metrics for profit. First, take a look at your data and see if there is a wide range of profitability results due to the diversity of your firm's offerings and client base. If so, set goals by practice area, region, and type of client. Set these goals a reasonable amount above the financial results the firm is striving to achieve.

Next, always have a break-even floor, so it is understood that any results below it yields negative profitability, where costs are not being covered for work on a particular matter. During the budgeting process, any projected results below this should not be given approval, notwithstanding other rationales. Additionally, it is helpful to provide actual average results in reports so that management and partners are confident that the goal metrics are anchored in reality and are achievable.

Internal reporting

Keep a "for-management's-eyes-only" list of all clients and matters, with profitability broken down to a granular level so that strengths and weaknesses can be identified quickly. These reports with profitability information should be sliced and diced in a few different ways, including by office, region, practice area, and by partner. This packet should include a separate report where profitability by fee arrangement type is a classification, which will help identify which types of fee arrangements are faring better than others, which could alter how fee arrangements are constructed. The overall reports should be shared with management on a monthly basis, as well as practice and office managing partners for their respective areas of responsibility. As long as individual partners have been trained on how to read the reports, they should receive them monthly as well on their respective books of business.

Roadshow

Hit the road! Since visibility is important, especially at larger firms, it is extremely valuable to travel to different offices and give presentations to groups of partners explaining a pricing and LPM team's capabilities and when they should be reaching out (as much as possible!). During this presentation (lunch meetings work well for maximum attendance), provide a high level explanation of how the profit methodology is calculated along with the goals (with a further explanation of different goals by practice groups as needed). Show sample reports and teach partners how to analyze them and understand what the key takeaways are.

One-on-one coaching

The mission of a pricing/LPM function is to be viewed by partners as an enabling group, helping them service their clients better while increasing profitability for the firm and the partners themselves. One-on-one meetings can go a long way towards creating relationships. Start with partners that are more inclined to be open to the messages and analysis that are being prepared, and schedule short, 30 minute sessions and walk into the meeting with the partner's top five or ten client matters and go through the statistics, including profitability.

The main levers for profit that should be analyzed are as follows.

The fee arrangement/discounting structure

Whether a fixed fee, discount, or other alternative fee arrangement, the pricing structure has the most direct impact on profitability, and should be thought through exhaustively, with a few different potential scenarios. A strong arrangement should yield strong profitability; a fair fee arrangement can be managed to be reasonably profitable through legal project management (LPM), but it's very difficult to yield strong profitability with a poor fee arrangement.

Staffing mix/leverage

At most large firms, non-partner attorneys are typically more profitable vs partners. This is more true in fixed fee situations since partners have higher rates. Though the most difference can be made by staffing a matter with a timekeeper from a lower rank, even within ranks (partners, counsel, associates, staff attorneys, paralegals), seniority makes a difference, and so the general approach should be to push the work down to the lowest resource that can complete the work efficiently with high quality. Utilizing LPM software, specific project plans should be drawn out for a matter either in its entirety or by quarter. When unforeseen duplication of work is being done, or there are unexpected timekeepers, or when there are higher level timekeepers billing time, the project manager and partners should be alerted. There is software that can raise flags if work is being completed by inappropriate timekeepers. There is also software available to help guesstimate how long certain tasks should take, and alerts set when this is exceeded by a certain amount.

Write-offs

Though it varies by firm, write-offs can be a significant source of profit erosion, and there may or may not be pushback when a partner decides to write off time. The causes vary – inefficiency, anticipated perception by client, going over a fixed fee, etc. These should all be investigated, and the lessons learned should be memorialized with the hope of them not being repeated.

Analyzing levers

These levers should be analyzed with an understanding of which one(s) can be improved to increase profitability for each matter. If the partner does not have the capability to make the changes, then the pricing/LPM professional should take the initiative of taking action and enlisting the assistance of others at the firm to put action steps into place to find an appropriate remedy.

Once the specific metrics to be improved are identified, close the loop by setting a goal of improving that metric within a set timeframe. For example, pushing work from a senior associate to a capable junior associate can be done quickly. Setting a new fee arrangement, though, can sometimes only be done once per year (or, as we're starting to see, every two years).

Calendar those goals and follow up with the partner to see how the metrics have changed, and have a discussion with the partner about the success or failure of making the aforementioned changes.

Client collaboration

Too often a successful negotiation is viewed as one where one side wins, the other side loses. The optimal goal should be a negotiation where both sides leave feeling that they have both won (but not overly won!). In this pursuit, transparency with clients can help. Profitability numbers are to be treated confidentially as an internal firm metric; regardless, sharing of actual profitability numbers is not constructive outside of context and relevance. But referring to profitability truthfully can help the pricing professional's negotiation with clients. Some examples:

> *"Offering this level of discounting will put us below our profitability goals, and management will not approve."*

> *"We can offer this fixed fee, but we will have to alter staffing to be able to meet our internal metrics."*

> *"We don't want our lawyers to avoid working on your matters because the discount we're providing you is greater than other clients in this practice area, since working on your matters will negatively impact the metrics of the individual lawyers."*

> *"Our utilization levels are high, and so we are not offering discounts for this type of work."*

"Though we have different fee arrangements with different clients, this level of discounting will put our overall metrics below that of other clients."
"The discounts we provided historically are not sustainable in the long run, and were provided at a time when your company was in financial distress to show our partnership and dedication to your business needs."

"The discounts we are providing are yielding results at the bare minimum we can afford."

"Because of our expertise, there are clients paying premiums for the work."

On the flip side, it's okay to offer clients concessions. Even if a client felt they received good value on a matter but internally the effort required was less than anticipated (and so the profitability was very high), offer the client a freebie – a subsequent matter with the exploratory phase written off, or 50 free hours, etc. Such gestures will go far in solidifying relationships.

Use successes as examples
Clients that prove to be very profitable can be used as examples to show how things should be done. Although specific numbers don't need to be mentioned, the aspects of a client relationship and how a matter is being managed successfully should be highlighted to others to serve as a model.

Fire the client!
This may sound unfathomable to some and an action of last resort, but it shouldn't be. When reviewing client financials, highlight the ones that fall below goal profitability and have an honest discussion about each one. No partner will want to give up clients, and the reasons typically provided for continuing to service unprofitable clients include that the client is a marquee client, has a strong brand name, is a longstanding client, serves as a referral source, the GC is a law school buddy of the managing partner, etc. Of course there are valid business justification reasons and utilization factors to consider, but getting rid of clients that are dragging down a firm's financials can free up opportunities for billing time on other more profitable clients, business development, and right-sizing headcount. If productive fee negotiations don't help improve the profitability of these unprofitable clients, refer the client to another

firm that would be happy to do their work – perhaps with a rate structure more compatible with the client's expectations, or simply because the law firm needs the additional revenue.

Chapter 9:
Leveraging profitability for action and results

By Madhav Srinivasan and Jim Foley, chief financial officer and pricing and legal project management director at Hunton Andrews Kurth LLP

The most interesting and productive part of the client matter profitability process is to leverage the framework and data for action and results – the action being positive behavior and the results being higher profitability. As a precursor to this effort, several foundational activities should already be in place – the adoption of a profitability focus by firm's senior management, selection of the most appropriate profitability model, and creation of the best reporting framework for sharing profitability data across the partnership.

Having embarked upon initiatives to drive profit-oriented behavior and increased profit dollars, our experience has shown that successful outcomes required a conjoint focus on all these key elements:

- Education;
- Opportunity analysis;
- Outreach;
- Smart pricing;
- Visibility; and
- Rewards.

Our program began with educating our entire firm on profitability, then engaging the pricing group for deep analytics and directly contacting partners to enable improvements on existing and new matters. These efforts were supported by creative pricing efforts, constant visibility across the firm, and linkages to annual rewards. The sum total of these integrated efforts was necessary to realize the full benefits of profitability in action. These elements are each described in detail below.

Education

Educating firm timekeepers and management on the profitability framework, its calculation, applicability, and reporting was a critical first step to gain support for future initiatives. We decided on a multimedia education program to present to all offices over an intense eight-week time period. We held multiple sessions in each of our larger offices and several video conferences with our smaller offices. We recorded a session and shared it on our firm intranet. The program covered key concepts such as the importance of profitability, model accounting calculations, reports and explanation, and data delivery. Each session was led by a senior finance manager who presented key concepts and many illustrative examples of how profitability levers can result in differing margin outcomes. We also included an interactive Q&A segment for each presentation.

We demonstrated that creative staffing models can lower the cost of legal services to the client while improving firm profitability – both as a percentage of fees and also in absolute dollars. The audience found this insight very useful as they considered future hiring.

By keeping detailed attendance of each session, we knew we had reached over 60 percent of the partnership in the first round of educational seminars. Our goal was to show that the model, including its various assumptions, was sound and directionally indicative. More so, we focused on the underlying drivers of substantial, rather than small margin differences, for example between 25 percent and 35 percent.

Our intense education efforts helped create a high degree of fluency with the profitability framework and a firmwide understanding of its importance and underlying action levers.

Opportunity analysis

Our pricing, legal project management and analytics group developed a client portfolio opportunity analysis framework. This framework ranked clients along the dimensions of current profitability and engagement volume. This allowed the team to identify clients and matters that could have the most impactful profit margin improvements. In effect, we were able to carve out a smaller set of clients where focused efforts could lead to maximum results. For this opportunity set, we analyzed pricing and fee models, staffing arrangements, budget monitoring status, write-off history, and collection issues. With this background and analysis we were able to highlight specific issues that could be enhanced, enabling the pricing team to collaborate with lead partners for concrete action plans to improve the profit margins over time.

This opportunity list of clients is being continually updated, and forms the basis for precise actions over the short-term. Owing to specific attention to such clients, the pricing group has been able to make many successful interventions with commendable results. In many cases, profitability has increased by several percentage points through smart leverage, better matter management, or creative rate proposals. Since the opportunity set consists of clients with the maximum possibility to improve, focused efforts have had a disproportionately higher impact on the overall firm.

Outreach

A critical part of creating results is to contact the partner who can make the changes needed to increase client matter profitability. We have an active outreach program to call the partners responsible for opportunity clients. We sit down and meet with these individual partners to review the profitability of their clients. Clients with low margins are identified and reasons for the low margins are explained. The same is done with clients that have better than average margins. In such discussions, we can compare these discounts and write-offs as a percentage of standard value to the firm average. A partner can quickly and clearly see whether the client or matter is above or below the firm average for discounts, write-offs, leverage, and resulting profit margin. While a broad education effort is useful to educate on key profitability concepts, the pricing group's outreach further explains and eliminates any confusion or uncertainty about specific client matter financial results. In many situations, a solid understanding can be accomplished with a simple interactive financial model that allows for different input values to produce varying fee and margin results.

With this deeper understanding, partners are encouraged to get more work from clients with better margins, avoid taking on more work from low margin clients, or make discrete changes to their underlying fee arrangement, staffing model, or matter management. Thus we actively work to improve the profitability of the firm's overall client portfolio.

An important tenet in profitability is that there is always some positive action that can be taken by the partner and the firm. For clients with heavily discounted rates that cannot be improved upon or with some other intractable fee arrangement, there often must be a change to the underlying staffing model. It is important to note that there is an internal marketplace for talent within a law firm and talent will gravitate towards more profitable work. Our task is to facilitate the power of this marketplace and encourage more profitable clients and matters while providing excellent client service. Many of our success stories result in improved profitability to the firm while reducing costs to the client.

We have seen, on occasion, a perceived tension between improving profit margins against increasing fee revenue. In the short-term, virtually all of a law firm's expenses are fixed and increasing market share regardless of margins is appealing to some partners. There may be a low opportunity cost due to underutilized lawyers and a psychic benefit to being busy rather than sitting idle. We believe this perception, given proper understanding, can be changed to show that smart efforts can lead to both increased fee volume and profit margins.

Smart pricing

Improving profit margins is not simply raising billing rates and sacrificing fee volume. We have discovered that a profitability focus at the front end allows us to develop creative pricing and fee models that can lead to increased revenue with acceptable profit margins. Many partners have been pleasantly surprised to learn that we can creatively and aggressively price new work that may, if managed well, produce acceptable levels of profitability. It is essential to fully understand the underlying drivers of these engagements at the outset. For example, on fixed fees or blended rate deals, good profitability can be realized only when engagement staffing is properly understood and managed. Effective matter management with clear and intuitive budgets helps keep the work on track.

One surprising result of the widespread use of our profit model has been more engagements with a success fee component. This has the dual advantage of greatly benefiting our clients and clearly aligning our mutual objectives. We are able to articulate creative fee deals with reasonable profitability that incorporate a success fee element, which, if realized, can result in an excellent outcome for the firm.

In certain situations, we are able to develop a fixed fee or blended rate price in anticipation of a future staffing model. For example, a practice area may be in the process of hiring associates, allowing us to price work with the assumption that those associates have already been hired. The work initially may be performed by more senior lawyers who eventually will be substituted by the additional junior lawyers. In the short-term, clients benefit from more senior lawyers without fully paying for their increased skills. Over the long-term, clients benefit from a legal team with a deeper bench of talent. The firm gains by efficient use of resources, which produce more than desired levels of profitability.

Visibility

Continuous and high visibility of profitability efforts keeps it fresh and top of mind for senior and operating management. Profitability metrics are disseminated on our intranet, presented on key financial reports, discussed in detail in operating meetings and displayed on partner metric dashboards. More so, timely feedback is essential. Annual, quarterly, and monthly reports with financial data are helpful, but, to be actionable, profitability results need to be communicated quickly and easily.

We developed a simple, easy to understand, one-page margin report for every single client and matter in the firm, which is posted on our firm intranet. Another useful graphic is a fee revenue waterfall, which starts with the standard value of time worked and ends with the final fee revenue received by the firm. Client matter profitability is also reported alongside fee revenue and realization on all standard reports, including those used in the partner compensation process, ensuring widespread visibility. Such efforts have proved very useful in maintaining focus on profitability improvement at all levels.

Rewards

There is a saying in law firm financial circles – all roads lead to partner compensation. Once partners see the prominence given to client matter profit margin results, they understand this initiative is fully supported by firm leadership and fully imbedded in the culture. Our partner compensation system is not formulaic, and profit margins are given due importance along with fee volume. Doing the right thing – timely and accurate timekeeping narrative, appropriate fee arrangements, prompt billing and collecting, effective matter management, and providing excellent client service – will continue to be rewarded. Such efforts should naturally result in attractive client matter profit margins. Client matter profitability thus becomes a quantitative measure of high quality partner behavior. All else being equal, two client portfolios with the same total fee revenue but quite different profit margins should lead to correspondingly different partner compensation results.

Summary

We started on our profitability journey five years ago by securing support from firm leadership, creating a profitability calculation that was fully accepted, designing systems and avenues to disseminate information, and educating the entire firm on profitability mechanics. The results of our initial efforts were a high degree of fluency with profitability metrics, a common language to discuss underlying drivers among leaders, and continuous reporting and visibility in key firm reports.

Our current efforts are designed to leverage this strong foundation for higher profitability results using all the elements described above. We have experienced good success in specific situations, where education, outreach, visibility, and feedback have produced visible increases in matter and client profitability. Overall, we have also seen improvements in the firm's total client portfolio. There is now a general receptivity in the firm towards initiatives to increase profitability, and the pricing group is engaged on multiple efforts to continue these promising results. Trends in the legal industry also favor an intense focus on firm profitability, which is recognized and fully supported by firm leadership. Our initiatives get more effective as we learn which aspects need to be strengthened, and we are continually finding new ways to maintain our focus on leveraging profitability for results and action.

www.ingramcontent.com/pod-product-compliance
Ingram Content Group UK Ltd.
Pitfield, Milton Keynes, MK11 3LW, UK
UKHW021848150926
8657IPUK00005B/148

9 781783 583720